Editor
Eric Migliaccio

Managing Editor
Ina Massler Levin, M.A.

Illustrator
Vicki Fraser

Cover Artist
Brenda DiAntonis

Art Production Manager
Kevin Barnes

Imaging
James Edward Grace
Rosa C. See

Publisher
Mary D. Smith, M.S. Ed.

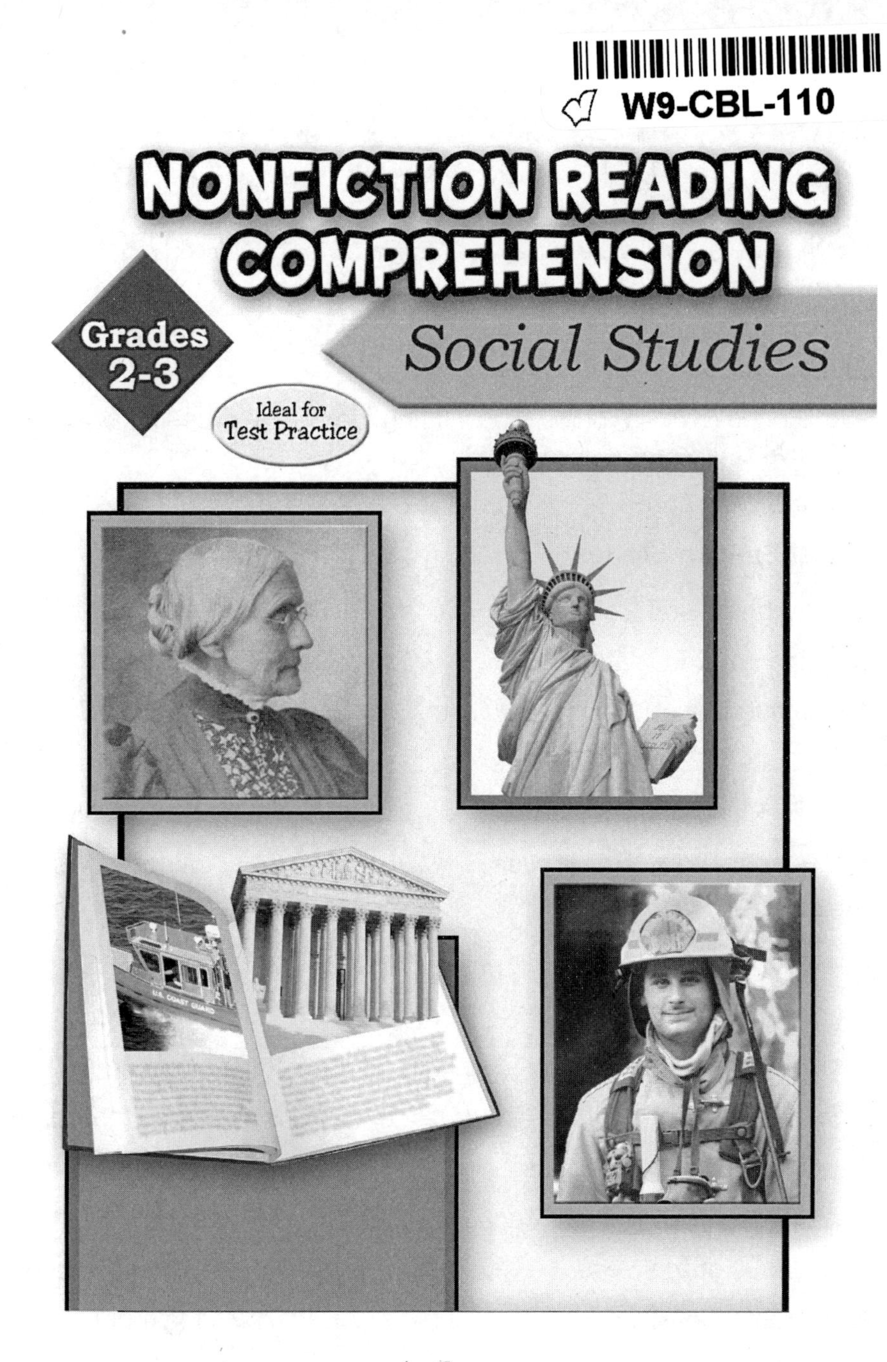

Author

Ruth Foster, M.Ed.

Teacher Created Resources, Inc.
12621 Western Avenue
Garden Grove, CA 92841
www.teachercreated.com

ISBN: 978-1-4206-8023-2

Reprinted, 2018
Made in U.S.A.

Table of Contents

Introduction

- ✻ **Social studies is thrilling.**
  Think of Dr. Alice Hamilton descending into a black hole over 800 feet (244 meters) deep in an elevator without walls to try to find out what was making miners sick.
- ✻ **It has changed our world.**
  Think of how the purchase of natural-resource-rich Alaska—"Seward's Icebox"—added 570,374 square miles (1,477,269 hectares) of land to the United States.
- ✻ **It affects our lives daily.**
  Think of how in 1916 the first supermarket with prepackaged food changed the way we shop.

Reading comprehension can be practiced and improved while coupled with social studies instruction. This book presents short, fascinating stories that focus on social studies topics. The stories were chosen to arouse curiosity; augment basic social studies facts taught at this grade level; and introduce a world of ideas, people, and events.

A page of questions follows each story. These questions will provide a child familiarity with different types of test questions. In addition, the practice they provide will help a child develop good testing skills. Questions are written so that they lead a child to focus on what was read. They provide practice for finding the main idea, as well as specific details. They provide practice in deciphering new and unknown vocabulary words. In addition, the questions encourage a child to think beyond the facts. For example, every question set has an analogy question where students are expected to think about the relationship between two things and find a pair of words with the same type of relationship. Other questions provide opportunities for the child to infer and consider possible consequences relevant to the information provided in the story.

The book is designed so that writing can be incorporated into every lesson. The level of writing will depend on what the teacher desires, as well as the needs of the child.

Lessons in *Nonfiction Reading Comprehension: Social Studies* meet and are correlated to the Mid-continent Research for Education and Learning (McREL) standards. They are listed on page 8.

A place for *Nonfiction Reading Comprehension: Social Studies* can be found in every classroom or home. It can be a part of daily instruction in time designated for both reading and social studies. It can be used for both group and individual instruction. Stories can be read with someone or on one's own. *Nonfiction Reading Comprehension: Social Studies* can help students improve in a multitude of areas, including reading, social studies, critical thinking, writing, and test-taking.

Using This Book

The Stories

Each story in *Nonfiction Reading Comprehension: Social Studies* is a separate unit. For this reason, the stories can be (but do not have to be) read in order. A teacher can choose any story that coincides with classroom activity.

Stories can be assigned to be read during social studies or reading periods. They can be used as classroom work or as supplemental material.

Each story is five paragraphs long. They range from 300–325 words in length. They are written at the second-grade level and have elementary sentence structure.

New Words

Each story includes a list of eight new words. Each of the new words is used a minimum of two times in the story. New words may sometimes have an addition of a simple word ending, such as *s, ed,* or *ing*. The new words are introduced in the story in the same order that they are presented in the new word list. Many of the new words are found in more than one story. Mastery of the new words may not come immediately, but practice articulating, seeing, and writing the words will build a foundation for future learning.

- A teacher may choose to have the children read and repeat the words together as a class.
- While it is true that the majority of the words are defined explicitly or in context in the stories, a teacher may choose to discuss and define the new words before the students begin reading. This will only reinforce sight-word identification and reading vocabulary.
- A teacher may engage the class in an activity where children use the new word in a sentence. Or, the teacher may use the word in two sentences. Only one sentence will use the word correctly. Children will be asked to identify which sentence is correct. For example, for the word *law,* the teacher might say,

  "A law is passed to give us rules to follow and keep us safe."

  "A law is what you will catch when you are sitting on a giraffe's back and fishing in Idaho."
- A teacher may also allow children to choose one new word to add to their weekly spelling list. This provides children with an opportunity to feel part of a decision-making process, as well as gain "ownership" over new words.
- A teacher may choose to have children go through the story after it is read and circle each new word one or two times.

Using This Book *(cont.)*

The Writing Link

A teacher may choose to link writing exercises to the social studies stories presented in the book. All writing links reinforce handwriting and spelling skills. Writing links with optional sentence tasks reinforce sentence construction and punctuation.

- ✻ A teacher may choose to have a child pick one new word from the list of new words and write it out. Space for the word write-out is provided in this book. This option may seem simple, but it provides a child with an opportunity to take control. The child is not overwhelmed by the task of the word write-out because the child is choosing the word. It also reinforces sight-word identification. If a teacher has begun to instruct children in cursive writing, the teacher can ask the child to write out the word twice: once in print and once in cursive.
- ✻ A teacher may choose to have a child write out a complete sentence using one of the new words. The sentences can be formulated together as a class or as individual work. Depending on other classroom work, the teacher may want to remind children about capital letters and ending punctuation.
- ✻ A teacher may require a child to write out a sentence after the story questions have been answered. The sentence may or may not contain a new word. The sentence may have one of the following starts:
    - I learned . . .
    - I thought . . .
    - Did you know . . .
    - An interesting thing about . . .

If the teacher decides on this type of sentence formation, the teacher may want to show children how they can use words directly from the story to help form their sentences, as well as make sure that words in their sentences are not misspelled. For example, for the first paragraph in the selection titled "Fishing on a Giraffe's Back" (page 10), possible sample sentence write-outs may be . . . .

"I learned that the state of Idaho passed a law about fishing for trout on a giraffe's back."

"I thought there weren't any laws about giraffes."

"Did you know that Idaho passed a law about fishing on a giraffe's back?"

"An interesting thing about Idaho is that it once passed as law about fishing on a giraffe's back."

This type of exercise reinforces spelling and sentence structure. It also teaches a child responsibility—a child learns to go back to the story to check word spelling. It also provides elementary report writing skills. Students are taking information in a story source and reporting it in their own sentence construction.

The Questions

Five questions follow every story. Questions always contain one main-idea, one specific-detail, and one analogy question.

- The main-idea question pushes a child to focus on the topic of what was read. It allows practice in discerning between answers that are too broad or too narrow.
- The specific-detail question requires a child to retrieve or recall a particular fact mentioned in the story. Children gain practice referring back to a source. They also are pushed to think about the structure of the story. Where would this fact most likely be mentioned in the story? What paragraph would most likely contain the fact to be retrieved?
- The analogy question pushes a child to develop reasoning skills. It pairs two words mentioned in the story and asks the child to think about how the words relate to each other. A child is then asked to find an analogous pair. Children are expected to recognize and use analogies in all course readings, written work, and in listening. This particular type of question is found on many cognitive functioning tests.

The remaining two questions are a mixture of vocabulary, identifying what is true or not true, sequencing, or inference questions. Going back and reading the word in context can always answer vocabulary questions. The inference questions are the most difficult for many students, but they provide practice for what students will find on standardized tests. They also encourage a child to think beyond the story. They push a child to think critically about how facts can be interpreted or why something works.

The Test Link

Standardized tests have become obligatory in schools throughout our nation and around the world. There are certain test-taking skills and strategies that can be developed by using this resource:

- Students can answer the questions on the page by filling in the circle of the correct answer, or you may choose to have your students use the answer sheet located at the back of the book (page 141). Filling in the bubble page provides practice responding in a standardized-test format.
- Questions are presented in a mixed-up order, though the main-idea question is always placed in the numbers one, two, or three slots. The analogy question is always placed in the three, four, or five slots. This mixed-up order provides practice with standardized-test formats, where reading-comprehension passages often have main idea questions, but these type of questions are not necessarily placed first.

The Test Link (cont.)

* A teacher may want to point out to students that often a main-idea question can be used to help a child focus on what the story is about. A teacher may also want to point out that an analogy question can be done any time, since it is not crucial to the main focus of the story.

* A teacher may want to remind students to read every answer choice. Many children are afraid of not remembering information. Reinforcing this tip helps a child to remember that on multiple-choice tests, one is *identifying* the best answer, not making up an answer.

* A teacher may choose to discuss the strategy of eliminating wrong answer choices to find the correct one. Teachers should instruct children that even if they can only eliminate one answer choice, their guess would have a better chance of being right. A teacher may want to go through several questions to demonstrate this strategy. For example, in the "Fishing on a Giraffe's Back" selection, there is the following question:

> 2. Laws for the entire country are
>
> (a) city laws (c) state laws
>
> (b) silly laws (d) federal laws

Students may not be sure what laws for the entire country are called, but after reading the answer choices, they may be able to eliminate the answer choice "(b) silly laws." They are left with the choices "city," "state," and "federal." At this point, a child may be able to eliminate the answer choice "(a) city laws," as the reading selection discusses that most laws that are silly laws are city laws. With two choices eliminated, either one of the remaining two answers has a good chance of being correct. The teacher can also remind children that there is the option of going back and finding the paragraph that contains the phrases "state laws" and "federal laws" in it.

The Thrill of Social Studies

The challenge of writing this book was to allow a child access to the thrills of social studies while understanding that many social-studies words or concepts are beyond a child's elementary-grade level. It is hoped that the range of stories and the ways concepts are presented reinforces basic social-studies concepts, all while improving basic reading-comprehension skills. It is also hoped that a child's imagination is whetted. After reading each story, a child will want to question and find out more.

Meeting Standards

Listed below are the McREL standards for Language Arts Level 1 (Grades K–2). All standards and benchmarks are used with permission from McREL:

McREL Standards are in **bold.** Benchmarks are in regular print. All lessons meet the following standards and benchmarks unless noted.

Uses grammatical and mechanical conventions in written compositions.

- Uses conventions of print in writing (All lessons where writing a new word or sentence option is followed.)
- Uses complete sentences in written compositions (All lessons where writing a complete sentence option is followed.)

Uses the general skills and strategies of the reading process.

- Understands that print conveys meaning
- Understands how print is organized and read
- Creates mental images from pictures and print
- Uses meaning clues
- Uses basic elements of phonetic analysis
- Uses basic elements of structural analysis
- Understands level-appropriate sight words and vocabulary
- Uses self-correction strategies

Uses reading skills and strategies to understand a variety of informational texts.

- Uses reading skills and strategies to understand a variety of informational texts
- Understands the main idea and supporting details of simple expository information

Fishing on a Giraffe's Back

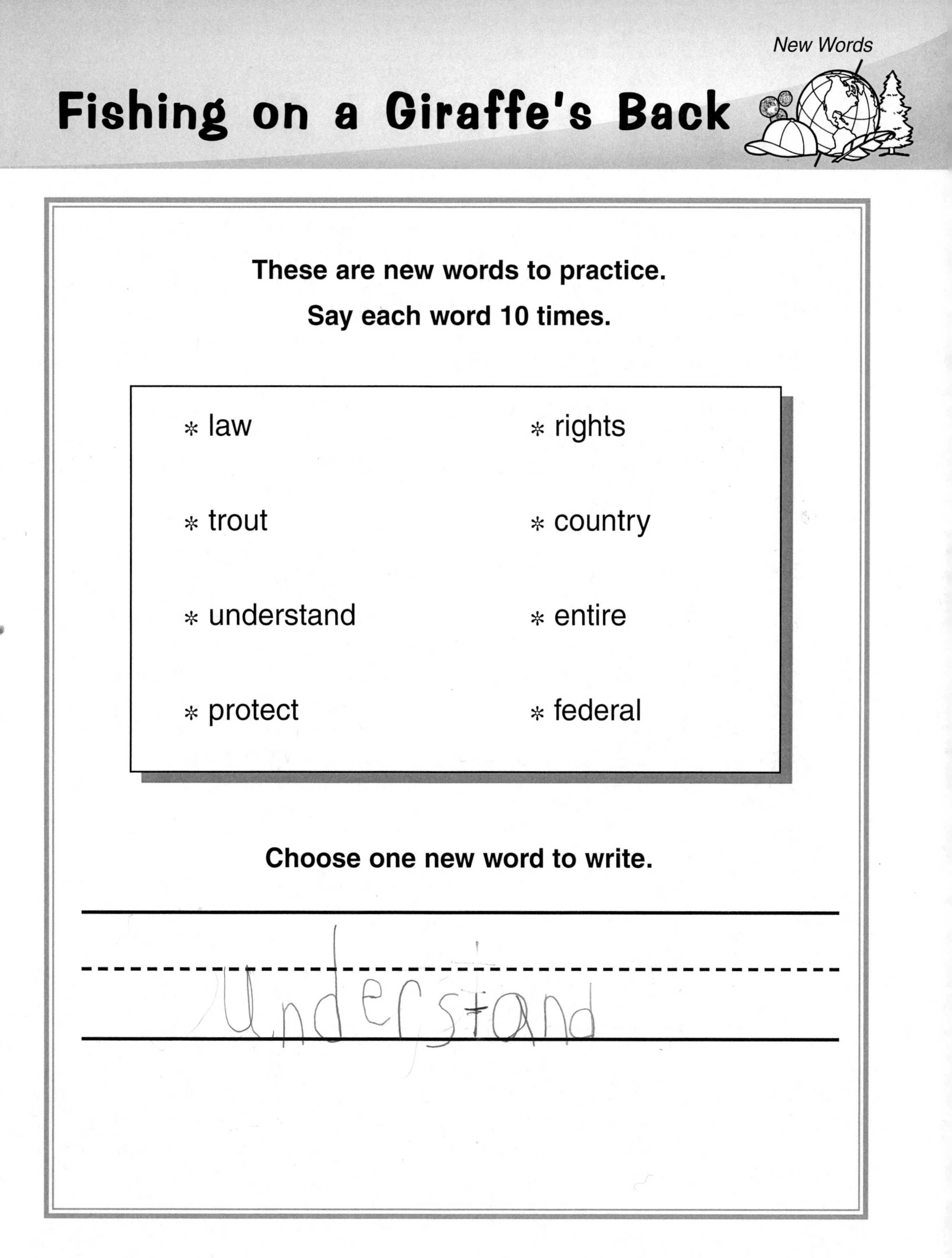

These are new words to practice.

Say each word 10 times.

* law	* rights
* trout	* country
* understand	* entire
* protect	* federal

Choose one new word to write.

Understand

Fishing on a Giraffe's Back

The state of Idaho passed a law. The law was about fishing for trout. A trout is a fish. The law said that you could not fish for trout if you were sitting on a giraffe's back. There are a lot of trout in Idaho. One can understand laws written to protect the fish. It is harder to understand the part about the giraffe! There are not a lot of giraffes in Idaho! Giraffes live in Africa. In the United States today, giraffes are only in zoos and special parks.

Laws are passed to keep us safe. Laws give us rules to follow. Laws help protect our rights. They keep us safe. We have the right to life. We have the right to be free. We have the right to be happy.

Every country has different laws. Some laws are for the entire country. These are called federal laws. Other laws are just for states. These are called state laws. Each state can pass its own state laws. Cities can pass their own laws, too. Some laws, when we look at them today, seem very silly. Most of these silly laws are not for the entire country. They are not federal laws. Most of them are city laws.

One city law was about horses. It said that it was against the law for horses to eat fire hydrants. Another city law was about lions. It said that it was against the law to take a lion to a movie theater. Another city law was about donkeys. It said that donkeys could not sleep in bathtubs.

One city law was about driving. The law said that you could not drive if you were asleep. One city law was about swimming. It said that you could not swim on dry land. Another city law was about ice cream. It said that you could not carry an ice-cream cone in your pocket.

Fishing on a Giraffe's Back

After reading the story, answer the questions.
Fill in the circle next to the correct answer.

1. This story is mainly about
   - (a) federal laws
   - (b) fishing for trout
   - (c) how laws can be changed
   - (d) how some laws seem silly today

2. Laws for the entire country are
   - (a) city laws
   - (b) silly laws
   - (c) state laws
   - (d) federal laws

3. Think about how the word *trout* relates to the word *fish*. What words relate in the same way?

   trout : fish

   - (a) law : city
   - (b) sun : light
   - (c) duck : bird
   - (d) giraffe : Africa

4. Why do you think a law was passed about taking a lion to a movie theater?
   - (a) Someone found a lion sleeping in his bathtub.
   - (b) Someone tried to take a lion to a movie theater.
   - (c) Someone wanted to make sure lions stayed in zoos.
   - (d) Lions are too big for the chairs in movie theaters.

5. When laws are passed to protect us, they are passed to
   - (a) to keep us safe
   - (b) to make us happy
   - (c) to give us rules to follow
   - (d) to make us part of a country

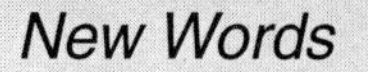

Bringing Land to Water

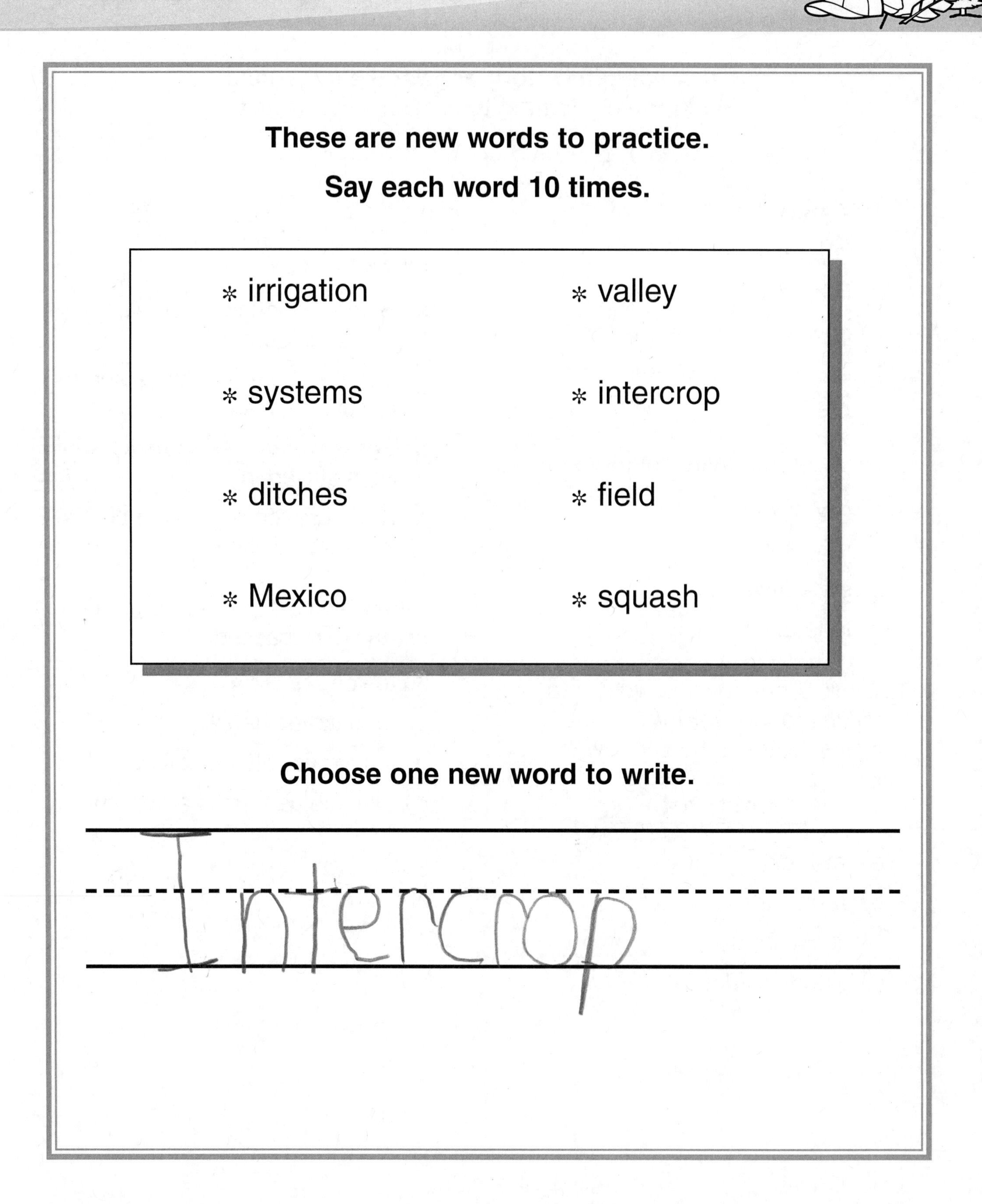

These are new words to practice.

Say each word 10 times.

- * irrigation
- * valley
- * systems
- * intercrop
- * ditches
- * field
- * Mexico
- * squash

Choose one new word to write.

Intercrop

Bringing Land to Water

Farmers plant crops. They plant crops for food. Crops need water to grow. Farmers set up irrigation systems. When you irrigate something, you get water to it. You dig ditches. Or, you set up a system of pipes. Water flows through the ditches and pipes. The water gets to the crops. With irrigation, a farmer can grow a lot more food. The farmer can water his or her crops when he or she needs to. The farmer does not have to wait for it to rain.

Long ago, people lived in the Valley of Mexico. It was where Mexico City is today. Lakes were at the bottom of the valley. Farmers wanted to irrigate. They wanted to set up irrigation systems. But there was a problem. The problem was that the lakes were at the bottom of the valley. How could they bring the water up to higher ground?

The people were smart. They did not bring water to the land. They brought land to the water! Farmers made floating beds. The beds were floating islands. First, the farmers made a raft. The raft was made out of branches or reeds. Next, the farmers took mud from the lake. They piled the mud on the raft. The mud made good, rich soil.

The farmers planted seeds on the mainland. Then, they planted the baby plants on the floating islands. They used tools. They made the tools out of wood and bone. The plants grew fast out in the lake. They had good, rich soil. They had water.

The farmers were smart. They learned to intercrop. When you intercrop, you put different plants in the same field. The farmers planted corn. They planted beans. They planted squash. Corn, beans, and squash were all planted on the same floating fields. The farmers knew that if they only planted corn, the soil would become poor. Intercropping corn, beans, and squash kept the soil good and rich.

Bringing Land to Water

After reading the story, answer the questions.
Fill in the circle next to the correct answer.

1. What did the farmers use for the bottom of the floating island?
   - (a) mud
   - (b) soil
   - (c) beds
   - (d) reeds

2. Why can a farmer grow a lot more food with irrigation?
   - (a) The farmer can plant more crops in ditches.
   - (b) The farmer can intercrop and keep the soil rich.
   - (c) The farmer does not have to wait for it to rain.
   - (d) The farmer does not have to use wood and bone tools.

3. This story is mainly about
   - (a) how to intercrop
   - (b) irrigation systems
   - (c) the Valley of Mexico
   - (d) farmers who brought land to water

4. Many farmers today grow corn and beans. They do not intercrop, but they change fields. One year a field will have corn. The next year it will have beans. A farmer probably does this
   - (a) to irrigate the corn and beans
   - (b) to keep the soil good and rich
   - (c) because he or she lives in the Valley of Mexico
   - (d) because he or she does not have a floating island

5. Think about how the word *rich* relates to the word *poor*. What words relate in the same way?

   rich : poor

   - (a) tool : bone
   - (b) different : same
   - (c) irrigation : water
   - (d) intercropping : corn

A Humbug Insect

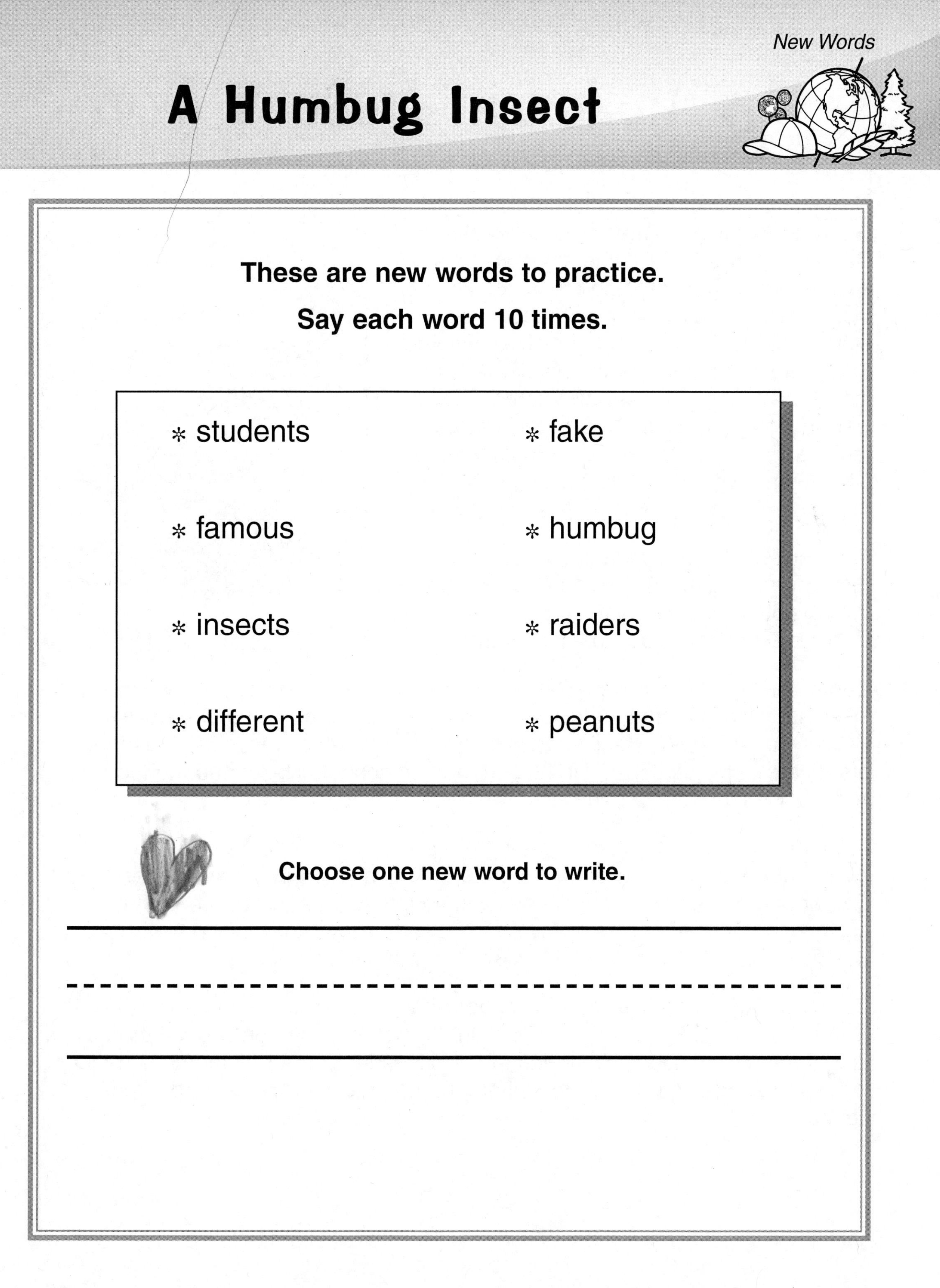

These are new words to practice.

Say each word 10 times.

- students
- fake
- famous
- humbug
- insects
- raiders
- different
- peanuts

Choose one new word to write.

A Humbug Insect

George Washington Carver was a teacher. Carver was known for something. He was known for being a very good teacher. He was also known for being very smart. Some students wanted to fool Carver. They wanted to trick their famous teacher. They got some insects. The insects were all different. They were not the same kind. Then, the students took parts from each insect. The parts were all different. Very carefully, the students put the parts together. They made a new insect!

George Washington Carver

The students took the fake insect to Carver. "Mr. Carver," they said, "We found an insect. We do not know what it is. Please help us, Mr. Carver. Can you tell us what insect this is?"

Carver looked at the insect. Carver was not fooled. He said, "I know what this insect is. This is a humbug insect!" A humbug is a trick. A humbug is a fake. Carver was not mad. He liked to joke with his students. In fact, Carver took great care of his students. He helped them in school. He helped them out of school. He lent them money.

Carver was born in 1864. He was born a slave. Slave raiders stole Carver and his mother. Carver's owner paid someone to find where the slave raiders took Carver and his mother. Only Carver was found. Carver never saw his mother again. Carver's father was a slave, too. Carver never knew his father. Carver was freed after the Civil War. He lived with the people who had owned him.

Carver worked hard. He went to school whenever he could. In college, he studied how to grow plants. Carter taught farmers how to grow good crops. He taught them ways to use what they grew. He is famous for all the uses he found for peanuts. Paper, ink, oil, and coffee are just a few things he made from peanuts.

A Humbug Insect

After reading the story, answer the questions.
Fill in the circle next to the correct answer.

1. Carver was freed

   ⓐ by his owner
   ⓑ after the Civil War
   ⓒ by the slave raiders
   ⓓ after he went to college

2. If you are famous,

   ⓐ you are fake
   ⓑ you work hard
   ⓒ you study plants
   ⓓ you are known for something

3. This story is mainly about

   ⓐ Carver
   ⓑ insects
   ⓒ a trick
   ⓓ growing crops

4. What can you tell about Carver from the story?

   ⓐ He wanted to be famous.
   ⓑ He wanted to help people.
   ⓒ He wanted to find new insects.
   ⓓ He wanted to fool his students.

5. Think about how the word *different* relates to the word *same*. What words relate in the same way?

   different : same

   ⓐ in : out
   ⓑ trick : fool
   ⓒ grow : crops
   ⓓ slave : raider

New Zealand Exchange Student

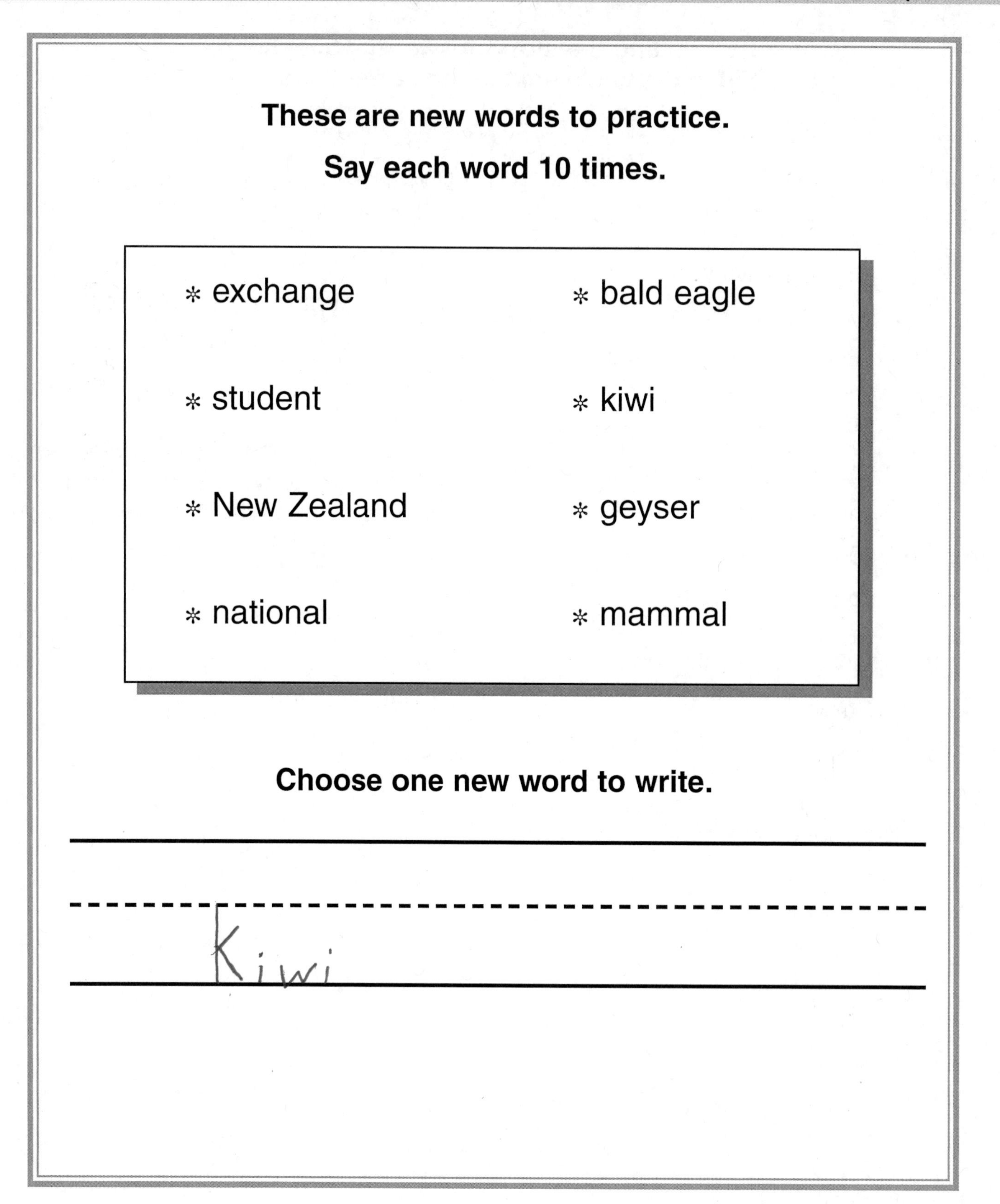

These are new words to practice.

Say each word 10 times.

- exchange
- student
- New Zealand
- national
- bald eagle
- kiwi
- geyser
- mammal

Choose one new word to write.

Kiwi

New Zealand Exchange Student

"I have the sign," said Lee. "I will hold it up. Kiri will know who we are because I have a sign." Lee was at the airport. Lee and her mother were picking up Kiri. Kiri was an exchange student. She was from New Zealand. She was going to stay with Lee and her family. She would stay for the summer.

Lee saw a girl come out of the gate. The girl smiled when she saw Lee's sign. She walked over to Lee. "Hi," said the girl. "I am Kiri. I am your exchange student. I have come to stay with you. I will learn about the United States. I will teach you about New Zealand. We will trade, or exchange, news. We will learn from each other."

Kiri saw how people in the United States lived. Both Lee and Kiri learned new things. Kiri learned the name of the national bird of the United States. The bird is the bald eagle. She liked the bald eagle's white head. Lee learned the name of the national bird of New Zealand. The bird is the kiwi. The kiwi cannot fly. It has a long bill. The bird's nostrils are on the tip of the bill! The kiwi lays only one egg. The egg is large. It is about one-third of the mother's weight!

Kiri and Lee learned how their countries are alike. Both of their countries have geysers. A geyser is a special spring. The spring shoots streams of boiling water and steam into the air. Only three countries have geysers. The United States has geysers. New Zealand has geysers. Iceland has geysers.

Lee learned that people called the Maoris settled New Zealand. They came long ago. They came in boats. Probably they came before 1,000 A.D.! Before the Maoris, all the mammals on New Zealand could fly! This was because the only mammals were bats! Non-flying mammals—like rats, cats, and sheep—came with people.

New Zealand Exchange Student

After reading the story, answer the questions.
Fill in the circle next to the correct answer.

1. When you exchange something, you
   - ⓐ keep it
   - ⓑ trade it
   - ⓒ stay for a summer
   - ⓓ learn something about it

2. What is not true about the national bird of New Zealand?
   - ⓐ It can fly.
   - ⓑ It lays one egg.
   - ⓒ It is called the kiwi.
   - ⓓ It has nostrils at the tip of its nose.

3. This story is mainly about
   - ⓐ birds
   - ⓑ New Zealand
   - ⓒ what Kiri learned
   - ⓓ Lee and an exchange student

4. How did mammals that cannot fly get to New Zealand?
   - ⓐ They swam to New Zealand.
   - ⓑ They fell out of an airplane.
   - ⓒ People brought them to New Zealand.
   - ⓓ The mammals grew there after people came.

5. Think about how the words *bald eagle* relate to the word *bird.* What words relate in the same way?

   bald eagle : bird

   - ⓐ egg : lay
   - ⓑ bat : mammal
   - ⓒ Maoris : boats
   - ⓓ Iceland : geyser

Mike Fink and the Mississippi

These are new words to practice.

Say each word 10 times.

* Mississippi	* waterways
* Gulf of Mexico	* engines
* keelboats	* current
* remote	* bull's-eye

Choose one new word to write.

Mike Fink and the Mississippi

The Mississippi River is a river. It is big. It is long. It starts in the north. It starts in Minnesota. It runs south. It flows through the United States. It empties into the Gulf of Mexico. It is 2,350 miles (3,780 kilometers) long. Lots of boats travel the Mississippi River. The boats carry people. The boats carry goods.

Keelboats used to go up and down rivers. Some would start in remote outposts. When something is remote, it is far away. There is nothing close to it. The keelboats would go for thousands of miles. They would travel a network of waterways. They would bring goods all the way down to the Gulf of Mexico. Then they would bring different goods back.

This was before there were planes and trains. This was before there were steamboats. This was before there were boats with engines. Without engines, the boats often had to be powered by hand. The boats could float down the river. They could not float going up. Men used poles. They would push on their poles. They would push the boats up the river. It was hard work. The boats had to go against the current.

Mike Fink was born in the late 1700s. He was a keelboat man. He was called king of the keelboat men. He was very strong. He traveled the waterways. He never let the strong current sweep his boat backward. There are lots of tales about Mike. Some are true. Some are tall tales.

One tall tale is about Mike and a shooting contest. He had three shots. He shot once. He hit the bull's-eye. "It's just a lucky hit," everyone said. Mike shot two more times. "You missed the whole target," people said. Then Mike made everyone look at the bull's-eye. There were three bullets in it! The bullets were all lined up as neatly as peas in a pod! "Mike can shoot the shell off an egg!" everyone said.

Mike Fink and the Mississippi

**After reading the story, answer the questions.
Fill in the circle next to the correct answer.**

1. This story is mainly about

   ⓐ rivers

   ⓑ Mike and a bull's-eye

   ⓒ a keelboat man and a river

   ⓓ boats on the Mississippi River

2. Where does the Mississippi River start?

   ⓐ Minnesota

   ⓑ Mississippi

   ⓒ Gulf of Mexico

   ⓓ Network of waterways

3. A tall tale is not

   ⓐ true

   ⓑ remote

   ⓒ powered

   ⓓ current

4. Think about how the word *up* relates to the word *down*. What words relate in the same way?

   up : down

   ⓐ egg : shell

   ⓑ river : water

   ⓒ remote : close

   ⓓ contest : bull's-eye

5. Why did we stop using keelboats on the Mississippi?

   ⓐ The river current is stronger today.

   ⓑ Goods are only carried down the river.

   ⓒ We do not need to carry goods anymore.

   ⓓ We can use engines to carry goods faster.

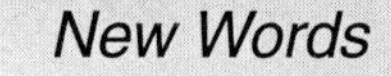

Not Enough Trees for a House

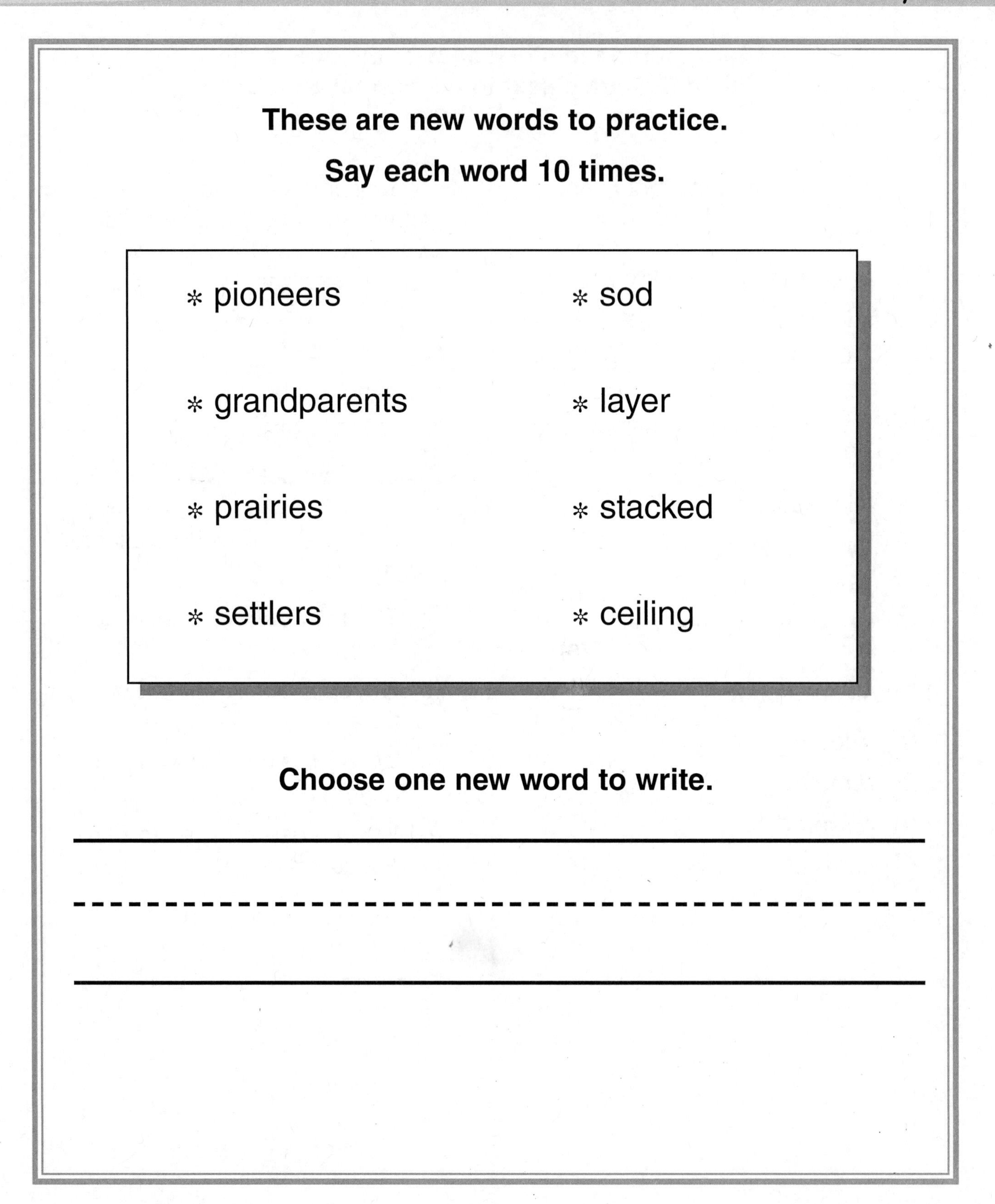

These are new words to practice.

Say each word 10 times.

* pioneers	* sod
* grandparents	* layer
* prairies	* stacked
* settlers	* ceiling

Choose one new word to write.

Not Enough Trees for a House

Long ago, people moved west. They were pioneers. The pioneers went west for free land. They wanted to settle down and make new homes. This was before you were born. This was before your parents were born. This was before your grandparents and great-grandparents were born! This was between the years of 1840 and 1890.

Many pioneers settled on the prairies. The prairies were flat. Tall grasses grew on them as far as the eye could see. People thought, "We can grow food here. We can plant lots of crops. This is a good place to make a home." But how could the settlers make a house? They needed a house to keep them safe. They needed a house to protect them from the weather.

A prairie is a land of few trees. How could the settlers make their homes when there were not enough trees? The settlers made their houses out of sod. Sod is dirt. It is the top layer of dirt. Sod is the layer that contains grass and roots. The sod was cut from the earth in large blocks. The blocks were stacked. They were stacked grass-side down. They were stacked like bricks. Thick, heavy walls were made with the sod blocks.

Most sod houses were just one room. They were about 20 feet (6 meters) long. They were about 16 feet (5 meters) wide. To make the roof, poles of willow or cottonwood were crisscrossed across the top of the walls. Then, a layer of sod was laid on the poles. The floors were dirt. It took one acre (.4 hectares) of sod to build a house this big.

Sod houses were cheap. They were fireproof. They were warm in the winter and cool in the summer. But sod houses were dark and musty. Dirt often fell from the ceiling. Sometimes bugs, mice, and other animals dropped from the ceiling! During heavy rains, water dripped from the roof.

Not Enough Trees for a House

After reading the story, answer the questions.
Fill in the circle next to the correct answer.

1. In sod houses, floors were
   - (a) dirt
   - (b) dark and musty
   - (c) made from blocks of sod
   - (d) crisscrossed with poles of willow or cottonwood

2. Pioneers made sod houses because
   - (a) they had lots of free land
   - (b) they used what they could find
   - (c) they built them long before you were born
   - (d) they liked them better than houses made out of wood

3. This story is mainly about
   - (a) pioneers
   - (b) sod houses
   - (c) building homes
   - (d) prairies with few trees

4. What is not a good thing about sod houses?
   - (a) They were cheap.
   - (b) They were fireproof.
   - (c) In the summer, they were cool.
   - (d) Dirt and animals fell from the ceiling.

5. Think about how the word *floor* relates to the word *ceiling*. What words relate in the same way?

   floor : ceiling

   - (a) many : few
   - (b) dirt : sod
   - (c) dark : musty
   - (d) tree : prairie

Where Was Ride?

These are new words to practice.

Say each word 10 times.

* thousand	* astronaut
* direction	* orbited
* countries	* gravity
* spaceship	* research

Choose one new word to write.

Where Was Ride?

Sally Ride could see far. She could look east. She could look west. She could look north. She could look south. She could see one thousand miles in any direction. She could see many countries. She could see them all at the same time. Where could Ride be? Where could she see one thousand miles in any direction? Where could she see many countries at the same time?

Sally Ride was in space. She was high above the Earth. She was in a spaceship. Ride was an astronaut. Astronauts travel. They travel into space. Ride was the first American woman to travel into space. She left Earth in 1983. The date was June 18th. She came back on June 24th. She traveled with four other astronauts. They traveled in the spaceship *Challenger*.

Challenger orbited Earth. When something orbits something, it goes around it. How long did it take *Challenger* to orbit Earth? It took only 90 minutes! *Challenger* orbited Earth sixteen times in just one day. This meant that Ride saw the sun rise and set sixteen times in one day!

Ride liked being an astronaut. She liked being in space. She liked how it felt when the force of gravity was not pulling her down. Without the force of gravity, she could float. She floated from place to place. One time she played a game. The game was to catch jellybeans. The jellybeans were floating, too! Ride had to catch the jellybeans with her mouth!

Sally Ride worked hard to become an astronaut. She went to school for many years. She had to have special training. The training was hard work. Ride was a good astronaut. She went into space two times. Ride then became a teacher. She wrote books. She helped direct space research. When you research something, you study it. You try to find out new things about it.

Where Was Ride?

After reading the story, answer the questions.
Fill in the circle next to the correct answer.

1. This story is mainly about
   - ⓐ spaceships
   - ⓑ space travel
   - ⓒ a woman astronaut
   - ⓓ astronaut training

2. What statement is true?
   - ⓐ Sally Ride wrote books in space.
   - ⓑ Sally Ride did not like being an astronaut.
   - ⓒ Sally Ride liked the force of gravity in space.
   - ⓓ Sally Ride could see one thousand miles in all directions.

3. Think about how the word *up* relates to the word *down*. What words relate in the same way?

   up : down

   - ⓐ rise : set
   - ⓑ orbit : around
   - ⓒ north : direction
   - ⓓ travel : spaceship

4. If you wanted to find out more about space travel, you might ______ it.
   - ⓐ float
   - ⓑ orbit
   - ⓒ travel
   - ⓓ research

5. How long was Ride in space?
   - ⓐ six days
   - ⓑ six months
   - ⓒ sixteen weeks
   - ⓓ sixteen years

One-Room School House

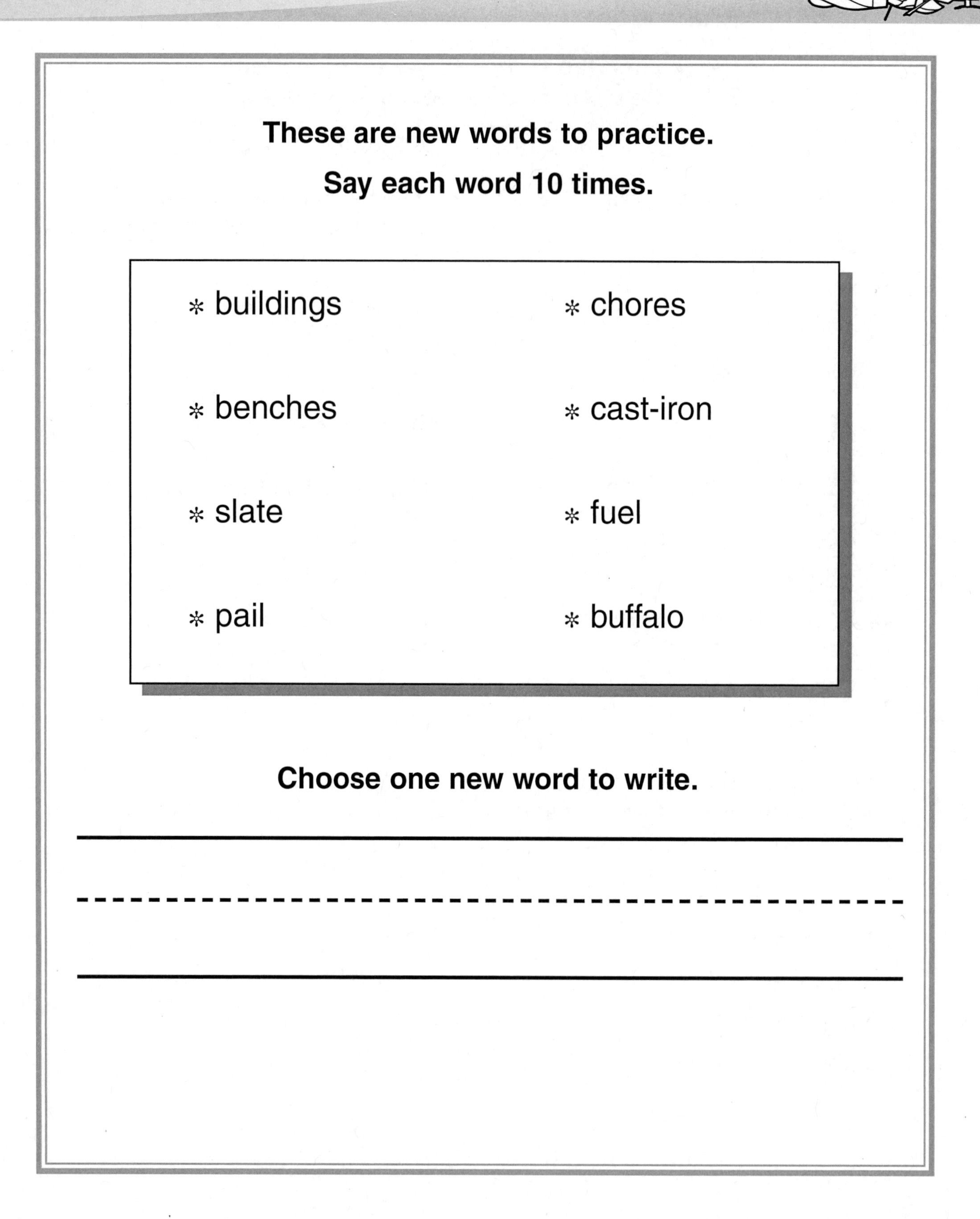

These are new words to practice.

Say each word 10 times.

- ✻ buildings
- ✻ chores
- ✻ benches
- ✻ cast-iron
- ✻ slate
- ✻ fuel
- ✻ pail
- ✻ buffalo

Choose one new word to write.

One-Room School House

Bea left for school. She did not take a school bus. There were no school buses. She did not ride in a car. There were no cars. Bea walked. She and her two brothers walked together. They walked three miles (5 kilometers) to get to school. She walked three miles (5 kilometers) back home.

This was long ago. This was before you were born. This was over 100 years ago. When settlers moved west, they built a school as soon as they could. The first schools were simple one-room buildings. They were made of sod or logs. The children sat on hard wooden benches. There were not any desks.

The younger children sat on the front wooden benches. The older children sat in the back. The teacher had a desk in front. When the teacher wanted to listen to lessons, he or she would call the students up to his or her desk. The girls sat on one side. The boys sat on another side. At recess, boys and girls played on different sides of the building.

Bea walked to school, but some children rode horses. Bea carried her slate to school. Her slate was like a small blackboard she could write on. Bea's oldest brother carried the dinner pail. He carried the dinner pail because he was the biggest. Bea's lunch and her brothers' lunches were in the dinner pail.

The children went to school only when they were not needed at home. Chores, such as plowing and planting, came first. A chore is a job you have to do. Children had chores at school, also. A cast-iron stove heated Bea's school. The children had to collect fuel for the cast-iron stove. Wood and buffalo chips were used as fuel. Buffalo chips are dried buffalo waste. The children found the chips in the grass. They carried them into the schoolhouse. They burned the chips in the stove.

One-Room School House

After reading the story, answer the questions.
Fill in the circle next to the correct answer.

1. This story is mainly about
   - (a) Bea and her brothers
   - (b) how children get to school
   - (c) chores children did at school
   - (d) what some schools were like long ago

2. How far did Bea walk to school and back every day?
   - (a) 3 miles (5 kilometers)
   - (b) 6 miles (10 kilometers)
   - (c) 12 miles (19 kilometers)
   - (d) 100 miles (160 kilometers)

3. Think about how the word *bench* relates to the word *sitting*. What words relate in the same way?

   bench : sitting

   - (a) chore : job
   - (b) fuel : wood
   - (c) younger : older
   - (d) slate : writing

4. What is not a chore?
   - (a) plowing
   - (b) planting
   - (c) playing at recess
   - (d) finding buffalo chips

5. Children used slates instead of
   - (a) cars
   - (b) paper
   - (c) desks
   - (d) lunch bags

A Law About Spinning

These are new words to practice.

Say each word 10 times.

* Massachusetts	* linen
* colony	* precious
* Europe	* harvested
* flax	* fibers

Choose one new word to write.

A Law About Spinning

A law was passed in Massachusetts Colony. This was before Massachusetts was a state. It was the year 1640. This was when people from Europe were coming to settle in America. The law was about children. What did the law say?

The law said that every child in the colony had to learn to spin. They had to learn how to spin flax. What is flax? Why did every child in the colony have to learn to spin flax? Early settlers could not buy clothes. They had to make their own. It was a lot of work. Children were needed to help with the work.

Early settlers made clothes out of linen. Linen is made from flax. Flax is a plant. It is a long and thin plant. Early settlers brought flax seeds from Europe. The seeds were precious. When something is precious, it is worth a lot. The settlers planted the precious seeds carefully.

spinning wheel

The young flax plants were tender. They could break easily. The settlers had to be careful when they weeded the plants. They did not want to break them. They worked facing the wind. This way, if they bent a plant, the wind could blow it back up. Children often weeded the plants. Often, they did not wear shoes. Children are small. If a barefoot child stepped on a plant, it would do less harm.

The flax was harvested when it was grown. Some seeds were saved for next year. Other seeds were pressed and used to make oil. The settlers beat the rest of the harvested plant. Beating the flax got rid of the soft part. Long, tough fibers were left. The fibers were like long, tough threads. The fibers were chopped and left to dry. The dried fibers were then spun into thread. A spinning wheel was used. After the thread was spun, it was bleached or dyed. It was woven into cloth. Finally, it could be made into clothes.

A Law About Spinning

After reading the story, answer the questions.
Fill in the circle next to the correct answer.

1. This story is mainly about
   - (a) the year 1640
   - (b) flax and clothes
   - (c) laws about children
   - (d) the Massachusetts Colony

2. Why did settlers beat the harvested flax plant?
   - (a) to get rid of the weeds
   - (b) to get its seeds for oil
   - (c) to get rid of the soft part
   - (d) to get its seeds for planting

3. When something is worth a lot, it is
   - (a) precious
   - (b) harvested
   - (c) facing the wind
   - (d) like long, tough threads

4. Think about how the word *grow* relates to the word *plant*. What words relate in the same way?

   grow : plant

   - (a) spin : thread
   - (b) law : children
   - (c) weed : barefoot
   - (d) Massachusetts : colony

5. Why did children often weed the flax plants?
   - (a) They were barefoot.
   - (b) They liked to weed more than they liked to spin.
   - (c) They would do less harm if they stepped on a plant.
   - (d) There was a law that said they had to weed the flax plants.

A Muddy Joke

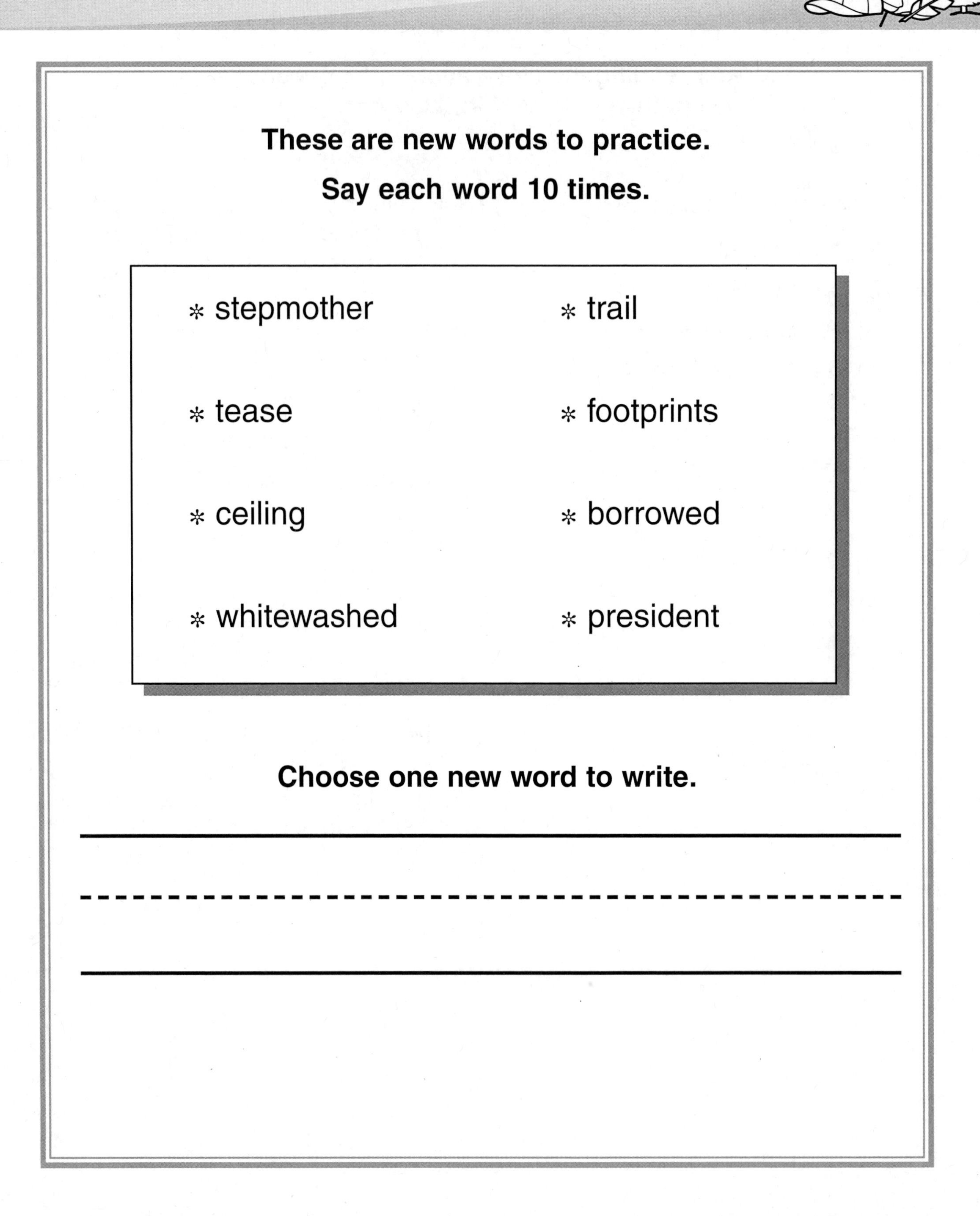

These are new words to practice.

Say each word 10 times.

- ⁎ stepmother
- ⁎ tease
- ⁎ ceiling
- ⁎ whitewashed
- ⁎ trail
- ⁎ footprints
- ⁎ borrowed
- ⁎ president

Choose one new word to write.

A Muddy Joke

Abe had a stepmother. Abe loved his stepmother very much. Abe's stepmother used to tease Abe. She would tease him about being tall. "You'd better wash your head," she would say. "Wash your head so you don't get the ceiling dirty."

Abe's stepmother liked things to be clean. Every spring, she cleaned their cabin. She cleaned the cabin from top to bottom. She even whitewashed the ceiling. Abe looked at the whitewashed ceiling. He looked at how clean and white it was. Then, Abe had an idea. Abe thought of a way to tease his stepmother. He would surprise his stepmother with a muddy joke!

Abe went to a little boy. "Step in the mud," he told the little boy. The little boy stepped in the mud. Then, Abe picked up the boy. He carried the boy into the house. Then, Abe turned the boy upside down. Abe held the boy up high so that the boy's feet touched the ceiling. Abe held the boy up as he walked across the ceiling. Soon, a trail of muddy footprints went right across the ceiling! Abe's stepmother was surprised when she saw the trail of muddy footprints. She laughed. She liked Abe's joke.

Abe's full name was Abraham Lincoln. He was born in 1809. He was born in Kentucky. His family was poor. They lived in a little cabin. It was made of logs. It had only one room. It had only one window. It had a dirt floor.

Abe's family moved to Indiana. His mother died when he was nine. Abe's father got married again. Abe's stepmother helped Abe. Abe didn't get to go to school very often, but Abe worked hard. He borrowed books. He read them by the firelight. He studied hard. He always returned the books he borrowed. Abe worked hard all of his life. He never stopped reading. He became president. He was the 16th president of the United States.

A Muddy Joke

**After reading the story, answer the questions.
Fill in the circle next to the correct answer.**

1. This story is mainly about
   - (a) Abe and his family
   - (b) Abe and a joke he played
   - (c) Abe and how he became president
   - (d) Abe and how he never stopped reading

2. What does Abe's stepmother do that shows she likes Abe's muddy joke?
   - (a) She laughed.
   - (b) She helped Abe.
   - (c) She was surprised.
   - (d) She whitewashed the ceiling.

3. What is not true about the cabin Abe was born in?
   - (a) It had a big room.
   - (b) It had a dirt floor.
   - (c) It had only one window.
   - (d) It was made out of logs.

4. Think about how the word *top* relates to the word *bottom*. What words most relate in the same way?

   top : bottom

   - (a) cabin : logs
   - (b) clean : muddy
   - (c) ceiling : floor
   - (d) feet : footprints

5. What do you think helped Abe become the president most?
   - (a) He was tall.
   - (b) He teased his stepmother.
   - (c) He didn't get to go to school very often.
   - (d) He worked hard and never stopped reading.

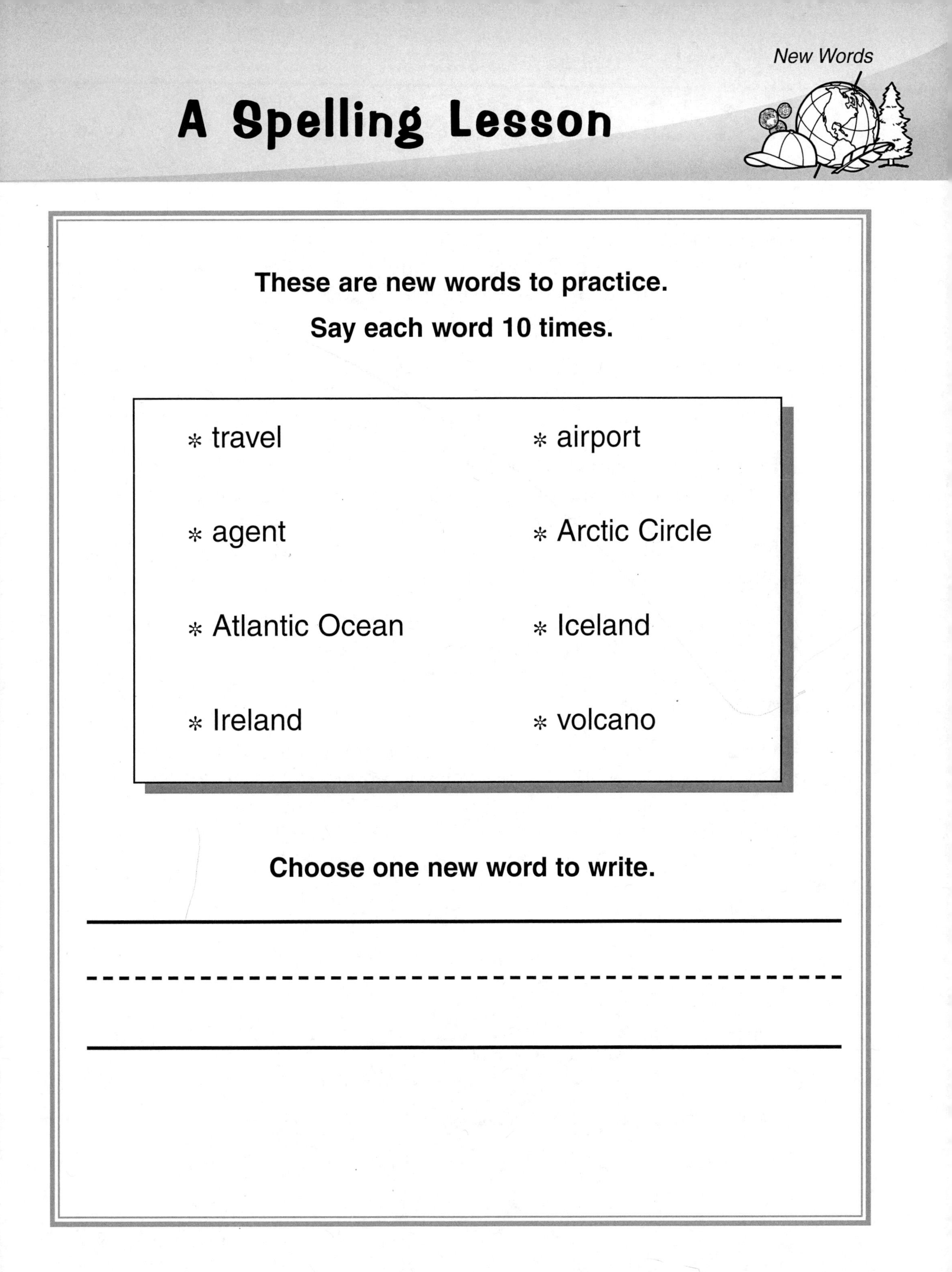

A Spelling Lesson

These are new words to practice.

Say each word 10 times.

- travel
- airport
- agent
- Arctic Circle
- Atlantic Ocean
- Iceland
- Ireland
- volcano

Choose one new word to write.

A Spelling Lesson

"I have a story about spelling," said Nat's Aunt Hi. Nat's Aunt Hi was a travel agent. A travel agent helps people go from one place to another. A travel agent buys tickets. He or she helps find travelers places to stay. "My story is about a traveler and a spelling lesson," said Aunt Hi.

"I got a note from a man," said Aunt Hi. "The note said, 'I want to go on a trip in June. I want to go to an island in the Atlantic Ocean. I want to go to Ireland." Aunt Hi got the man tickets. She found the man places to stay.

At the airport, the man handed his ticket to a ticket agent. The agent said, "The line is over there! Hurry!" The man got in the line. He got on the plane. He did not look at any signs. He slept on the plane. He woke up when the plane landed. When he left the airport, he was very surprised. It was the middle of the night. Still, it was light out! The sun was up!

The man was on an island. The island was in the Atlantic Ocean. Only, the island was not Ireland! The island was north of Ireland. It was near the Arctic Circle! It was so close to the Arctic Circle that in June there was no dark night. The man was in Iceland!

"The man was not angry," said Aunt Hi. "He was not angry because there are volcanoes on Iceland. He got to see a volcano erupt. The man told me this when he came to check the note he had sent me. He said, 'The surprise trip was a lesson. The lesson is that I must write neatly. Spelling is important. If your 'r' looks like a 'c,' you may end up on the wrong island in the Atlantic Ocean!'"

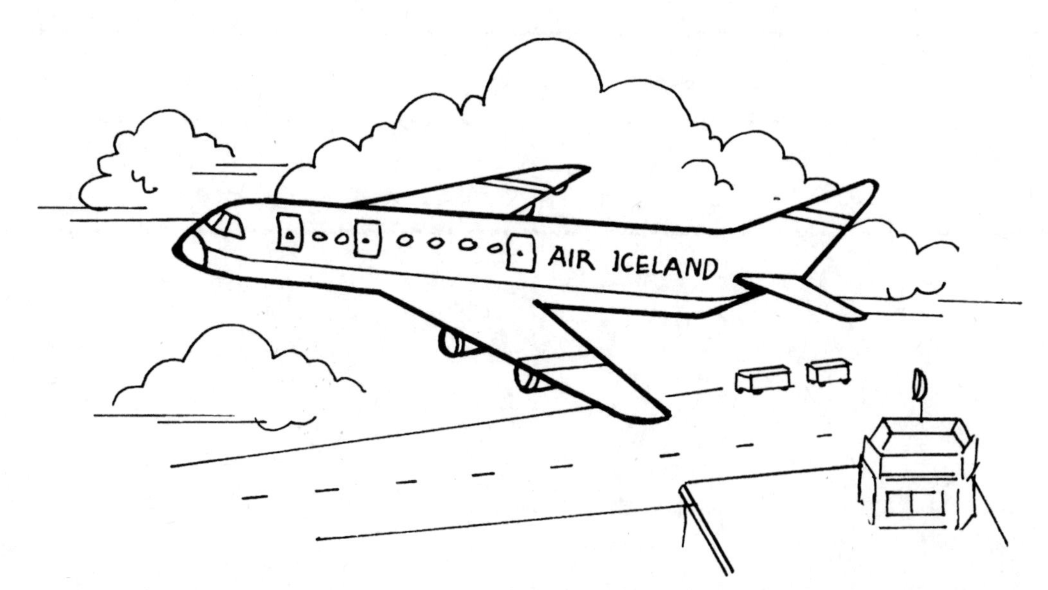

A Spelling Lesson

After reading the story, answer the questions.
Fill in the circle next to the correct answer.

1. This story is mainly about

   ⓐ a travel agent
   ⓑ why we have spelling lessons
   ⓒ islands in the Atlantic Ocean
   ⓓ how a man went to the wrong island

2. What answer is true about the islands in the story?

   ⓐ Both islands have volcanoes.
   ⓑ Both islands are in the Atlantic Ocean.
   ⓒ Ireland is closer to the Arctic Circle than Iceland.
   ⓓ In June, the days are longer in Ireland than Iceland.

3. When you travel, you

   ⓐ see volcanoes
   ⓑ go to an airport
   ⓒ go from one place to another
   ⓓ write a note to a travel agent

4. Think about how the word *close* relates to the word *near*. What words relate in the same way?

close : near

   ⓐ angry : mad
   ⓑ travel : stay
   ⓒ plane : airport
   ⓓ island : Atlantic

5. The next time the man wants to go on a trip, he will most probably

   ⓐ go to Ireland and not sleep on the plane
   ⓑ go to Iceland in June to see a volcano erupt
   ⓒ make sure his ticket is to where he wants to go
   ⓓ not use Aunt Hi as a travel agent because she cannot spell

The Ojibwe and Maple Sugar

These are new words to practice.

Say each word 10 times.

* Ojibwe	* pouch
* maple	* trough
* centuries	* container
* birch	* syrup

Choose one new word to write.

The Ojibwe and Maple Sugar

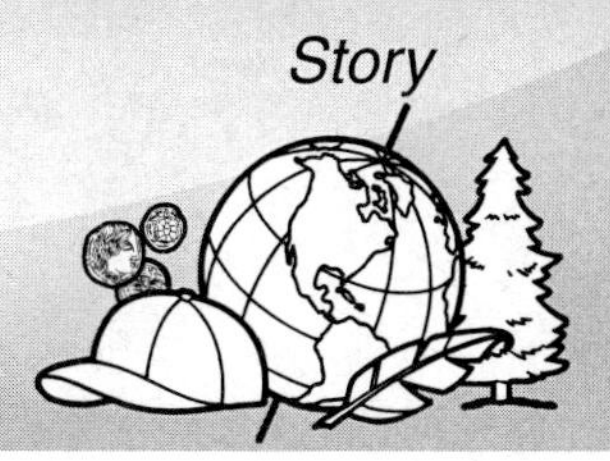

The Ojibwe are Native Americans. They live in the north. They live around the Great Lakes. They have made maple sugar for centuries. A century is 100 years. For centuries, the Ojibwe set up sugar camps. The sugar camps became their home for several weeks. They stayed in the sugar camps while they made maple sugar.

The Ojibwe worked together. They tapped the maple trees. How did they tap the trees? First, they drove a cedar chip into the trunk of the tree. Second, they cut a gash in the bark. The gash was just above the chip. Third, they put a birch bark pouch beneath the chip. Maple sap dripped into the birch bark pouch.

The Ojibwe emptied the birch bark pouches when they were full. They emptied the pouches into a large trough. A trough is a long, narrow, open container. The trough was made out of birch bark or moose hide. Next, the Ojibwe boiled down the sap. How was the sap boiled down? The Ojibwe could not put the trough over the fire. A birch-bark or moose-hide container would burn up if it were put over the fire!

The Ojibwe heated rocks. They put hot rocks inside the trough. They used hot rocks to boil the sap. The sap boiled night and day. It boiled until it thickened. It thickened into maple syrup. Some syrup was eaten, but most of it was boiled some more. It was boiled into maple sugar. The sugar was brown. The sugar was crumbly.

Trading changed the way the Ojibwe made sugar. The Ojibwe traded for iron kettles. The iron kettles could be put over the fire. This made boiling down the sap easier. The Ojibwe traded some sugar for blankets and household goods. They stored the rest of the sugar in containers or pits. The pits were lined with birch bark. Then, the Ojibwe could eat their stored sugar all year long.

The Ojibwe and Maple Sugar

After reading the story, answer the questions.
Fill in the circle next to the correct answer.

1. What did the Ojibwe trade for that changed the way they made sugar?

   ⓐ blankets
   ⓑ containers
   ⓒ iron kettles
   ⓓ household goods

2. This story is mainly about

   ⓐ how the Ojibwe lived
   ⓑ something the Ojibwe made
   ⓒ a hat the Ojibwe traded for
   ⓓ how the Ojibwe worked together

3. What answer is in the right order for making maple sugar?

   ⓐ store the sugar, drive a chip, cut a gash
   ⓑ cut a gash, empty filled pouch, drive a chip
   ⓒ drive a chip, cut a gash, put pouch beneath chip
   ⓓ put pouch beneath chip, cut a gash, store the sugar

4. A century is

   ⓐ one hundred years
   ⓑ around the Great Lakes
   ⓒ a long, narrow, open container
   ⓓ a pouch made out of birch bark or moose hide

5. Think about how the word *child* relates to the word *skin*. What words relate in the same way?

   child : skin

   ⓐ tree : bark
   ⓑ maple : sap
   ⓒ sugar : brown
   ⓓ trough : container

Guts Enough Not to Fight Back

These are new words to practice.

Say each word 10 times.

* baseball	* temper
* player	* together
* guts	* cruel
* enough	* fought

Choose one new word to write.

Guts Enough Not to Fight Back

Branch Rickey wanted a baseball player. The baseball player needed something. The player needed "guts enough not to fight back." Jackie Robinson was that player.

Robinson was born in 1919. He was born in Georgia. His grandparents had been slaves. He was a hard worker. He knew how to keep his temper. Robinson was a player with guts enough not to fight back.

Jackie Robinson

Before Robinson, black and white players did not play together. Whites played on their own teams. Blacks played on their own teams. Some people wanted to change this. They wanted to make baseball a true team sport. Rickey was the president of a white team. The team was the Brooklyn Dodgers. Rickey asked Robinson to play on his team. The year was 1945.

Many people were mad. They were angry. They did not want black and white players on the same team. Rickey knew that people would be mad. He knew they would be cruel. He knew they would fight. That is why Rickey needed a player with "guts enough not to fight back."

What would happen if Robinson fought back? If Robinson fought back, it would prove to some people that white and black players could not get along. It would prove that white and black players could not be on the same teams. People were very cruel to Robinson. They hit him. They threw balls at him. They called him names. They sent him mean letters. They tried to stick their sharp shoe spikes into him. Robinson did not lose his temper. He did not hit back. He did not call anyone names. Robinson fought back in a different way. He fought back by playing even harder. He hit lots of balls. He stole bases. He helped his team. His team began to win and win. Robinson became a hero. He showed everyone that baseball is a true team sport. Today, baseball players of all colors play together. Robinson had the guts to show people how.

Guts Enough Not to Fight Back

After reading the story, answer the questions. Fill in the circle next to the correct answer.

1. What year did Rickey ask Robinson to play on his team?

   ⓐ 1919
   ⓑ 1945
   ⓒ 1954
   ⓓ 1991

2. This story is mainly about

   ⓐ baseball
   ⓑ a team sport
   ⓒ baseball players of all colors
   ⓓ a man with guts enough not to fight back

3. What did Robinson do to fight back in a different way?

   ⓐ He threw balls.
   ⓑ He played harder.
   ⓒ He lost his temper.
   ⓓ He called people names.

4. From the story you can tell that in a true team sport

   ⓐ all players need to be the same skin color
   ⓑ some players cannot be on the same team
   ⓒ all players have shoes with sharp spikes
   ⓓ the skin color of the players does not matter

5. Think about how the word *mad* relates to the word *angry*. What words relate in the same way?

   mad : angry

   ⓐ mean : cruel
   ⓑ black : color
   ⓒ temper : fight
   ⓓ baseball : team

Ambulance of the Seas

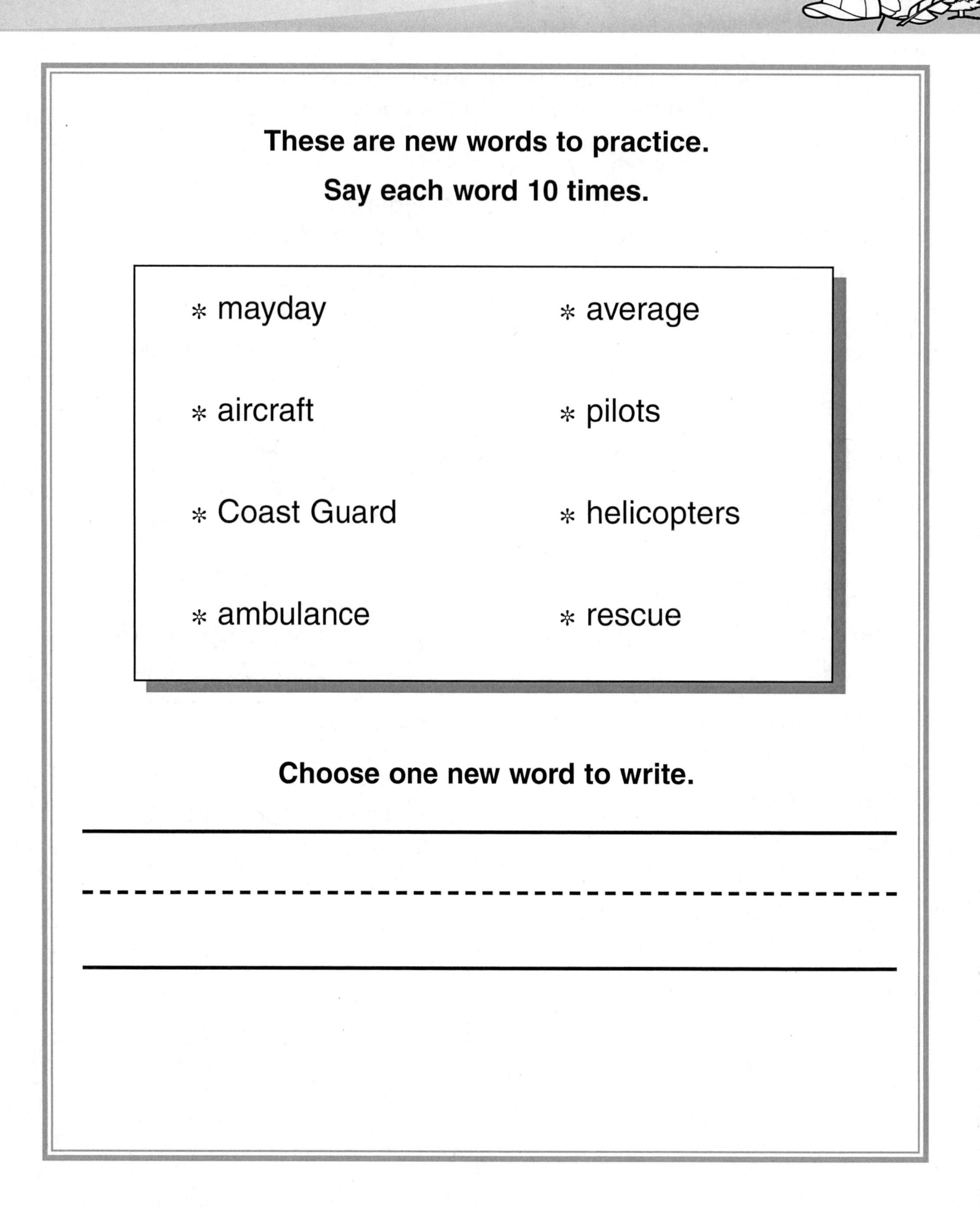

These are new words to practice.

Say each word 10 times.

* mayday
* average
* aircraft
* pilots
* Coast Guard
* helicopters
* ambulance
* rescue

Choose one new word to write.

Ambulance of the Seas

A big storm hits. A boat starts to sink. The words "Mayday, mayday!" can be heard on the radio. What do the words mean? The words mean "help." "Mayday" is the word used to call for help by ships and aircraft. Who can help out in the water? Who can help in a big storm?

The Coast Guard is part of the United States Armed Services. The Coast Guard works in U.S. waters. Its job is to protect the United States. Some people call the Coast Guard the police of the seas. The Coast Guard can stop ships. It can search ships. It can look for people breaking the law.

The Coast Guard does more than police U.S. waters. It does more than look for people breaking the law. The Coast Guard saves people. When the Coast Guard hears "Mayday," they come at once. They come fast. They help anyone who is in need. This is why they are called "the ambulance of the seas." Like a land ambulance, they get people help fast. On an average day, the Coast Guard saves ten lives. On an average day, the Coast Guard helps more than 190 people.

People in the Coast Guard have to know how to do many things. Some members of the Coast Guard know how to fly. They are pilots. They pilot different types of aircraft. They pilot planes. They pilot helicopters. The pilots fly over the ocean. They look for ships in trouble. They look for people in the water.

Some members are rescue swimmers. Rescue swimmers go into the water. Sometimes they drop out of helicopters. They swim to people in the water. They put the people in rescue baskets. The baskets are connected to the helicopters. One Coast Guard member has to lower the basket. Then, he or she has to carefully raise it. Other Coast guard members are firefighters. Even in the water, ships can catch on fire.

Ambulance of the Seas

After reading the story, answer the questions.
Fill in the circle next to the correct answer.

1. This story is mainly about

   (a) ambulances
   (b) helping people
   (c) the Coast Guard
   (d) calling for help

2. The Coast Guard is part of the

   (a) United States Armed Services
   (b) United States Police Services
   (c) United States Ambulance Services
   (d) United States Firefighting Services

3. Think about how the words *Coast Guard* relate to the word *water*. What words relate in the same way?

   Coast Guard : water

   (a) pilot : fly
   (b) police : land
   (c) fire : firefighter
   (d) helicopter : aircraft

4. Which statement is true?

   (a) Some Coast Guard members are pilots.
   (b) All Coast Guard members are firefighters.
   (c) All Coast Guard members are rescue swimmers.
   (d) Some Coast Guard members are ambulance drivers.

5. How many lives do Coast Guard members save on an average day?

   (a) 1
   (b) 10
   (c) 190
   (d) 1900

A Supreme Court Case

These are new words to practice.

Say each word 10 times.

- * Supreme
- * Court
- * justices
- * president
- * Senate
- * oath
- * equal
- * citizens

Choose one new word to write.

A Supreme Court Case

A case was before the Supreme Court. The Supreme Court is the highest court in the land. The Court has nine members. The members are called justices. The members serve for life. Justices are not elected. They are chosen.

First, the president chooses someone. Then, the person goes before the Senate. The Senate votes on the president's choice. If the vote is "yes," the person takes an oath. An oath is a vow. It is a promise. The person vows to "do equal right to the poor and to the rich."

The Court takes about 150 cases a year. It does not have time for more. It takes cases that the lower courts do not agree on. It takes cases that are important to many people. One case was about a nursing school. The school was paid for by the state. The nursing school was for women. It did not want to let in men. The school wanted to keep men out.

The justices listened. They listened to both sides. Should men be let into the school? Should men not be let into the school? The Court decided. The Court said the school had to let men in. The school could not keep men out. We have a law, the Court said. The law was about equal rights. The law said that all citizens have equal rights. Men are citizens. Women are citizens. Men and women are all equal.

One justice said that just because nurses usually have been women, it doesn't mean that men can't be good nurses. Who was this justice? This justice was Sandra Day O'Connor. O'Connor is a woman. She was the first woman on the Supreme Court! Before, only men had been on the Supreme Court. O'Connor knew that just because justices usually have been men, it didn't mean women can't be good justices. O'Connor was born in 1930. She became a justice in 1981. She said she would retire in 2005.

Sandra Day O'Connor

A Supreme Court Case

**After reading the story, answer the questions.
Fill in the circle next to the correct answer.**

1. This story is mainly about

   (a) nurses
   (b) O'Connor
   (c) the Supreme Court
   (d) laws and equal rights

2. What is not true about the Supreme Court?

   (a) It has nine members.
   (b) It has justices that are elected.
   (c) It takes cases that are important to many people.
   (d) It takes cases that the lower courts do not agree on.

3. What year did the Supreme Court get its first female justice?

   (a) 1909
   (b) 1930
   (c) 1981
   (d) 1993

4. Think about how the word *boys* relates to the word *girls*. What words relate in the same way?

   boys : girls

   (a) oath : vow
   (b) men : women
   (c) equal : same
   (d) justice : member

5. Why did the Court say that the nursing school had to let in men?

   (a) because nurses were usually women
   (b) because Justice O'Connor was a woman
   (c) because the justices had taken an oath
   (d) because we have a law that all citizens are equal

A House Without Doors

These are new words to practice.

Say each word 10 times.

- ✻ Pueblo
- ✻ Southwest
- ✻ temperature
- ✻ freezing
- ✻ adobe
- ✻ covered
- ✻ ladders
- ✻ stories

Choose one new word to write.

A House Without Doors

Long ago, many houses did not have doors. Why would someone make a house without a door? The houses were called pueblos. The Pueblo people made the houses. The Pueblo people lived in the Southwest. The Southwest is a dry, desert land. During the day, it is hot. In the summer, it is often more than 100 degrees F (38 degrees C)! It is cool at night. In winter, temperatures are often freezing.

The Pueblos needed houses to fit the land. They needed houses that could keep them cool when the temperature was hot. They needed houses that could keep them warm when it was freezing cold. They needed houses they could make with what was at hand. They made houses out of stone or adobe bricks. Adobe is heavy clay. Adobe mud was used to hold the stones and bricks together.

Pueblo walls were thick. The thick walls kept out the summer heat. In the winter, the thick walls kept in the heat. The floors were hard clay. Often, there were no windows. If there were windows, they were small. They were high up. The roofs were made from sticks. The sticks were covered with adobe.

Round holes were left in the roofs. People used the holes to go in and out of their homes! The people put ladders down the holes. They used the ladders to climb up and down. When the ladders were pulled in, it was hard for things to get inside. The holes could be covered with flat stones. With the holes covered, the house was protected when it was not being used.

Many homes were built together. They were built on top of each other. Some buildings were five stories high! Each story was set back from the one below it. Ladders were used to get from floor to floor. Some upper stories did have low doors. With the low doors, you could enter from the roofs of the lower floors.

A House Without Doors

**After reading the story, answer the questions.
Fill in the circle next to the correct answer.**

1. This story is mainly about
   - (a) the Southwest
   - (b) houses the Pueblos made
   - (c) doors that were round holes
   - (d) why the Pueblos needed ladders

2. What did the Pueblo people do to protect their homes when they were not being used?
   - (a) pulled in the ladder
   - (b) built the homes on top of each other
   - (c) covered the round roof holes with flat stones
   - (d) made the homes with stones or thick adobe bricks

3. If a Pueblo home did have a door, it was most probably
   - (a) a high door
   - (b) a round door
   - (c) on an upper floor
   - (d) on the bottom floor

4. Think about how the word *hot* relates to the word *cold*. What words relate in the same way?

hot : cold

   - (a) low : high
   - (b) round : hole
   - (c) adobe : brick
   - (d) floor : story

5. Why did the Pueblo people make their homes from stones and adobe?
   - (a) They could find stones and adobe in the Southwest.
   - (b) They could build their homes on top of each other.
   - (c) They could build houses with little windows and thick walls.
   - (d) They could pull their ladders in and make it hard to get inside.

Pictures that Teach

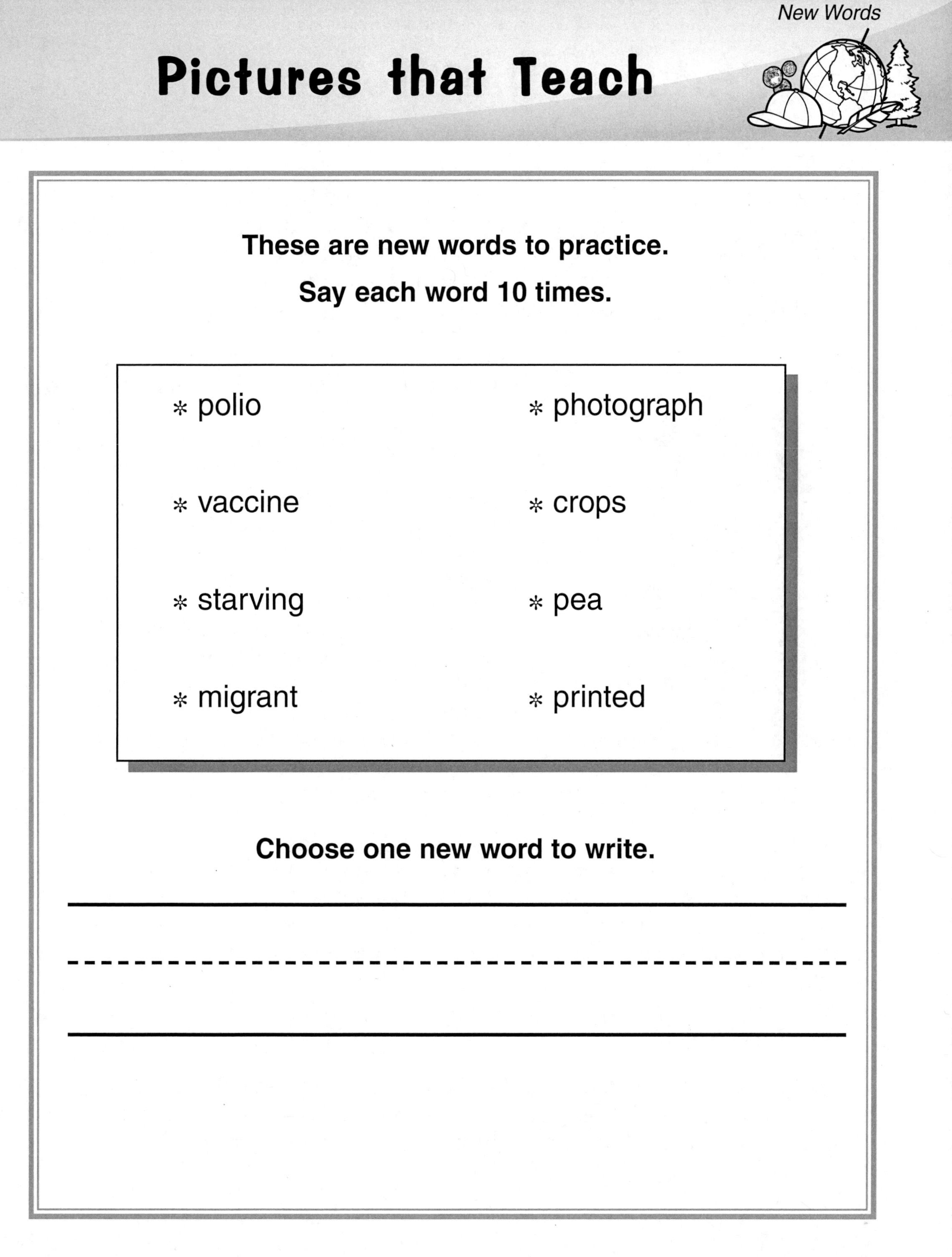

These are new words to practice.

Say each word 10 times.

* polio	* photograph
* vaccine	* crops
* starving	* pea
* migrant	* printed

Choose one new word to write.

Pictures that Teach

Children were mean to Dorothea Lange. They called her "Limpy." Lange limped because she got sick when she was a child. She got sick with polio. Today, we have a polio vaccine. The vaccine stops us from getting polio. Lange was born in 1895. She got polio when she was seven. We did not have the polio vaccine then. Lange limped for the rest of her life.

Dorothea Lange

Lange was strong. She did not let mean words stop her. She did not let her limp stop her. She did want she wanted. She wanted to be a photographer. She wanted to take pictures. Lange's pictures were special. They were teaching pictures. They taught us how some people lived. Today, Lange's pictures are famous. The pictures help us learn about the past.

One time Lange took a picture of a mother. The mother was very poor. She had no money. She was holding a baby. Two small children leaned on her. The mother had no food. Her children were starving. The mother was a migrant worker. She did not have a home. She lived in a tent. She moved from job to job.

Lange took the photograph to show people what life was like for migrant workers. Many people became migrant workers during the 1930s. This was a hard time. Many stores closed. People lost their jobs. Then, it did not rain in many states. Farms failed. Dust blew everywhere. To earn money, people became migrant workers. They moved to where the farms did not fail. They went from farm to farm. They planted crops. They picked crops. The migrant mother had gone to pick peas. But the pea crop had frozen. There was nothing to pick. There was no work.

The photograph was printed in the newspaper. A story about the picture was printed, too. It told about the starving pea-pickers. The picture made people want to do something. Food was sent to the pea-pickers' camp.

Pictures that Teach

After reading the story, answer the questions.
Fill in the circle next to the correct answer.

1. When was Lange born?
   - (a) 1825
   - (b) 1859
   - (c) 1865
   - (d) 1895

2. This story is mainly about
   - (a) how we learn from pictures
   - (b) polio and why Lange limped
   - (c) a migrant mother who was starving
   - (d) a photographer and a picture she took

3. Why couldn't the mother in the picture pick peas?
   - (a) She had polio.
   - (b) Her children needed her.
   - (c) All the peas were frozen.
   - (d) Migrant workers had picked them.

4. Which is not a crop?
   - (a) peas
   - (b) tents
   - (c) apples
   - (d) oranges

5. Think about how the word *poor* relates to the word *money*. What words relate in the same way?

   poor : money

   - (a) small : baby
   - (b) migrant : move
   - (c) starving : food
   - (d) photographer : pictures

True Stories About Coins

These are new words to practice.

Say each word 10 times.

- coin
- metal
- value
- barter
- bronze
- colonists
- mint
- government

Choose one new word to write.

True Stories About Coins

A coin is a piece of metal money. Each coin has a certain value. It is worth a certain amount. Early coins helped trade. Early coins helped traders all around the world. How could coins help trade? With coins, traders did not have to barter. They did not have to pay for goods with other goods. They could pay money. People were willing to take coins because their value was the same. It was the same from one place to the next.

Some coins were not round. Early coins in China were shaped like tools. They were shaped like small hoes. They were shaped like small knives. They were shaped like the tools the people in China used to barter! The coins were made out of bronze. Bronze is a kind of metal. The knife coins were about six inches (15 centimeters) long.

Early American colonists often used Spanish dollars. The Spanish dollars were large coins. They were made out of silver. They were called "pieces of eight." There were two reasons why the early American colonists used the "pieces of eight."

The first reason was that they were not allowed to mint coins. When you mint a coin, you make it. You mold it out of metal. Only governments can mint coins. Early colonists did not yet have their own government. The second reason was that Britain put limits on how many coins could go to the colonies. They let only a certain number of coins go.

It was easy to make change with Spanish dollars. To make change, you chopped the coin! You chopped it into pie-shaped pieces! It made eight pie-shaped pieces. The pieces were called bits. Two bits were worth a quarter of a dollar. Four bits were worth a half-dollar. Today, some people still say "two bits." They say "two bits" to mean a quarter of a dollar. A quarter of a dollar is 25 cents.

True Stories About Coins

After reading the story, answer the questions.
Fill in the circle next to the correct answer.

1. What were early coins in China made of?
   - ⓐ tools
   - ⓑ silver
   - ⓒ bronze
   - ⓓ pie-shaped pieces

2. This story is mainly about
   - ⓐ early coins
   - ⓑ Spanish dollars
   - ⓒ American colonists
   - ⓓ bartering and coins

3. Why were people willing to trade goods for coins?
   - ⓐ Early coins were large.
   - ⓑ Only governments could mint coins.
   - ⓒ The pieces of silver could be broken into bits.
   - ⓓ The coins had the same value from one place to the next.

4. Which statement is true?
   - ⓐ "Two bits" are worth half a dollar.
   - ⓑ People in China used Spanish dollars.
   - ⓒ Early colonists could make their own coins.
   - ⓓ Britain limited the number of coins the colonists could have.

5. Think about how the word *bake* relates to the word *cake*. What words relate in the same way?

   bake : cake

   - ⓐ tool : hoe
   - ⓑ mint : coin
   - ⓒ money : value
   - ⓓ silver : metal

The Great Lakes

These are new words to practice.

Say each word 10 times.

* Huron	* Superior
* Ontario	* glaciers
* Michigan	* basins
* Erie	* connected

Choose one new word to write.

The Great Lakes

"Help!" said Asa. "I need to remember something. I need to remember the names of the Great Lakes. I need to remember what Great Lake is the biggest, too. How can I remember the names? How can I remember what lake is biggest?"

Asa's Uncle Jo laughed. He said, "I will help you. There is a trick. Think of the word 'homes.' All you have to do is remember 'homes.' 'Homes' has five letters. There are five Great Lakes. Each letter stands for one lake. The 'h' stands for Lake Huron. The 'o' stands for Lake Ontario. The 'm' stands for Lake Michigan. The 'e' stands for Lake Erie. The 's' stands for Lake Superior."

Asa said, "'H' for Huron. 'O' for Ontario. 'M' for Michigan. 'E' for Erie. 'S' for Superior. Put them together, and they spell 'homes.' Uncle Jo, I like your trick. It is easy to remember 'homes.' Now, it is easy to remember all the Great lakes."

The Great Lakes

Uncle Jo said, "It is easy to remember which lake is biggest, too. If you are superior, you are higher in rank. You are better. You are excellent. Lake Superior got its name because it is the biggest lake. It is superior in size. In fact, Lake Superior is more than the biggest Great Lake. It is the biggest fresh-water lake in the whole world!"

What formed the Great Lakes? Huge sheets of ice called glaciers formed them. The glaciers were big and heavy. Some of them were two miles (3 kilometers) thick! The glaciers slowly moved across the land. As they moved, they carved deep basins in the land. As the glaciers melted, fresh water filled the basins. Lake Superior is the deepest of the Great Lakes. It is the coldest, too. All the Great Lakes are connected. The Great Lakes are connected to the Atlantic Ocean, too. They are connected by the St. Lawrence Seaway.

The Great Lakes

After reading the story, answer the questions.
Fill in the circle next to the correct answer.

1. What word did Asa's uncle tell her to remember?

   ⓐ helps
   ⓑ homes
   ⓒ hooks
   ⓓ highs

2. What is not true about Lake Superior?

   ⓐ It is the warmest Great Lake.
   ⓑ It is the deepest Great Lake.
   ⓒ It is connected to the other Great Lakes.
   ⓓ It is the biggest fresh-water lake in the world.

3. This story is mainly about

   ⓐ five lakes
   ⓑ Asa and her uncle
   ⓒ how lakes are formed
   ⓓ how the Great Lakes are connected

4. Why can trade goods loaded on a boat on Lake Superior go all the way across the Atlantic Ocean?

   ⓐ Lake Superior is higher than the other lakes.
   ⓑ Big and heavy glaciers carved out basins long ago.
   ⓒ The Atlantic Ocean is not as cold as Lake Superior.
   ⓓ The St. Lawrence Seaway connects the lakes to the ocean.

5. Think about how the word *water* relates to the word *lake*. What words relate in the same way?

   water : lake

   ⓐ "h" : Huron
   ⓑ ice : glacier
   ⓒ basin : carved
   ⓓ superior : best

Great-Grandpa and the Mine

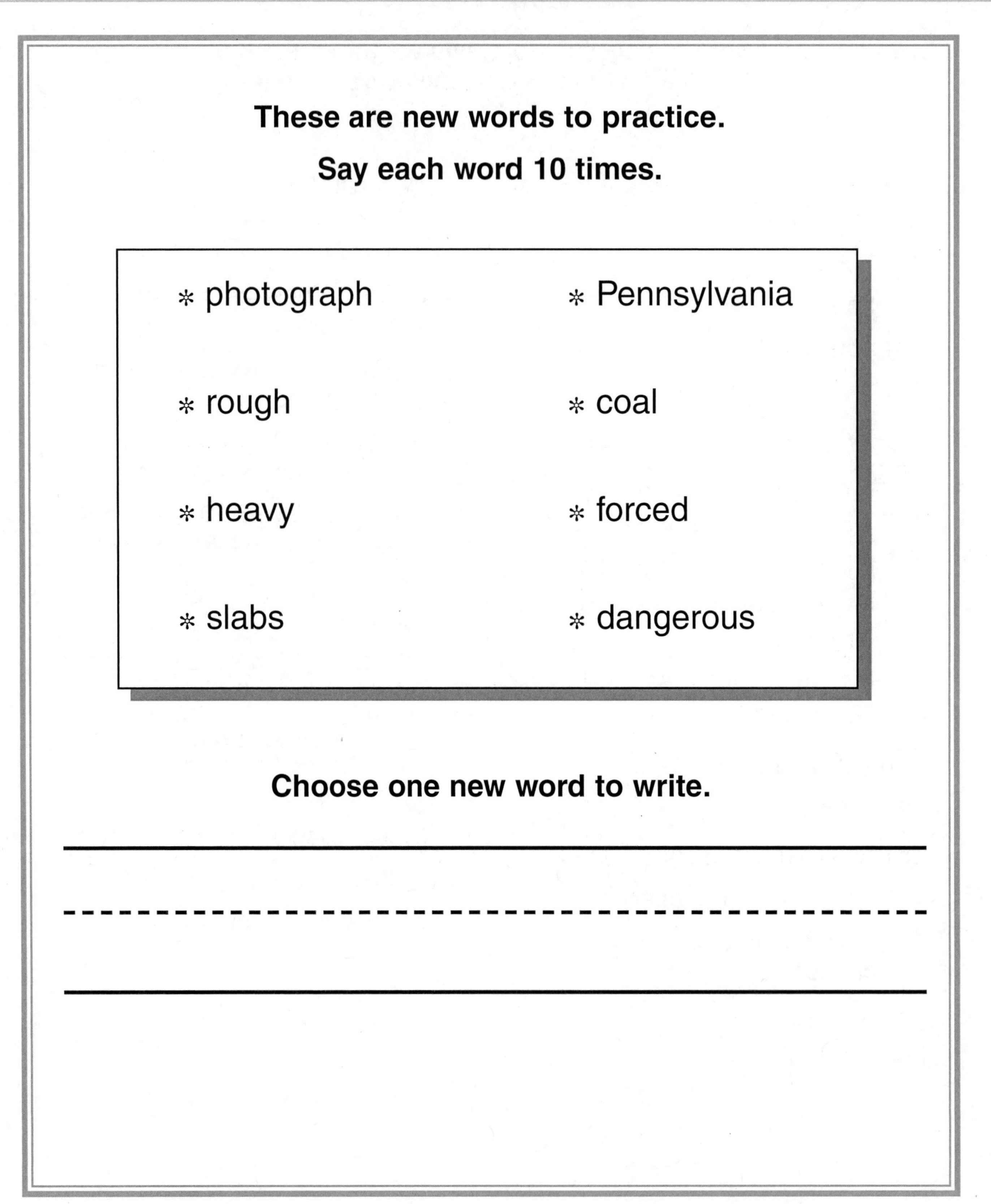

These are new words to practice.

Say each word 10 times.

* photograph	* Pennsylvania
* rough	* coal
* heavy	* forced
* slabs	* dangerous

Choose one new word to write.

Great-Grandpa and the Mine

Pat said, "This photograph is very old. It is black and white. It is a picture of a boy. He is wearing overalls. He has on a cap. He is sitting on a wooden box in front of a huge door. The door is made of rough, heavy, wooden slabs. A track goes under the door. The track is made of two iron rails. Dad, who is the boy? Where is he? Why isn't he in school?"

Pat's Dad said, "Written on the photograph is '1900, Pennsylvania.' Long ago, before you were born, your great grandpa was a coal miner. He worked in the mines in Pennsylvania. He was only eight years old. He did not go to school. Instead, he went deep under the ground. He earned money for his family.

"By looking at old photographs, we can learn what life was like long ago. Young boys had to sit by heavy doors made of rough slabs all day. If the doors were not shut, the miners would not have good air to breathe. Huge fans forced fresh air from above the ground into the mines. When the air hit the closed doors, it was forced into side tunnels. It went into the tunnels where the miners were working.

"All day your great-grandpa listened for coal cars. The cars rode on the track. They were filled with coal. When a car got close, your great-grandpa opened the door. If he did not open the door in time, the car would crash. It was very dangerous. After the cars went through, he closed the door tightly.

"It was very dark. Great-grandpa's only light came from a tiny lamp. He said that he used to trap rats for fun. Trapping rats helped him stay awake. Today we have laws about children working. Children today have to go to school. They cannot work in dangerous mines. The photograph of great-grandpa helps us remember why we made those laws."

Great-Grandpa and the Mine

After reading the story, answer the questions.
Fill in the circle next to the correct answer.

1. Why did Pat's great-grandpa work in the mines?

   ⓐ He was eight years old.
   ⓑ He didn't want to go to school.
   ⓒ He wanted to go deep under the ground.
   ⓓ He needed to earn money for his family.

2. What did Pat learn about his great-grandpa that he could not learn from the photograph?

   ⓐ that his great-grandpa wore overalls
   ⓑ that his great-grandpa worked in 1900
   ⓒ that his great-grandpa trapped rats to stay awake
   ⓓ that his great-grandpa had a wooden box to sit on

3. This story is mainly about

   ⓐ Pat and his school
   ⓑ how one boy stayed awake
   ⓒ what it is like in Pennsylvania
   ⓓ learning about the past from a photograph

4. What would happen if Pat's great-grandpa didn't shut the door tightly?

   ⓐ Coal cars would crash into them.
   ⓑ The track would not go under the door.
   ⓒ Fresh air would not get to side tunnels.
   ⓓ He would have to listen carefully all day.

5. Think about how the word *dark* relates to the word *light*. What words relate in the same way?

   dark : light

   ⓐ shut : open
   ⓑ ground : mine
   ⓒ listen : close
   ⓓ dangerous : crash

Sitting Bull

These are new words to practice.

Say each word 10 times.

* Lakota	* struggled
* swollen	* allies
* neighing	* unite
* raging	* protect

Choose one new word to write.

Sitting Bull

Sitting Bull crossed the river. He crossed it with a small band of his fellow Lakota. They set up camp. During the night, it rained. It rained and rained. The river became swollen with water. It flooded. Water ran over its banks.

In the morning, a woman cried for her horse. Everyone could see her horse. It was pawing the ground. It was neighing. But there was a problem with the horse. The horse was across the river. How could the woman get her horse? How could she cross the big, swollen river?

Sitting Bull did not say a thing. Quietly, he walked upstream. He had to go about half a mile (.8 kilometers). He made his way through the raging water. It was a hard trip. Still, Sitting Bill struggled across. He went to the neighing horse. He talked gently to it. Then, he got on its back. The horse listened to Sitting Bull. It stepped into the swollen river. The horse struggled against the raging water. It was swept downstream. Sitting Bull stayed calm. About half a mile (.8 kilometer) downstream, they reached the other side.

Sitting Bull was born in 1831. He was a Native American. He was born in present-day South Dakota. Sitting Bull was a member of the Lakota tribe. Lakota means "us people" or "allies." Allies are friends. Allies are people who unite together. Allies protect each other. The Lakota are also known as the Sioux.

Sitting Bull was a good hunter. He killed his first buffalo when he was very young. He was only ten years old. He killed the buffalo while riding on his horse. He killed it with a bow and arrow. Sitting Bull grew up to be a chief. He was a good chief. He fought to unite and protect his people all of his life.

Sitting Bull

After reading the story, answer the questions.
Fill in the circle next to the correct answer.

1. This story is mainly about
   - ⓐ buffalo
   - ⓑ a Lakota chief
   - ⓒ saving a horse
   - ⓓ Native Americans

2. How old was Sitting Bull when he killed his first buffalo?
   - ⓐ 9
   - ⓑ 10
   - ⓒ 18
   - ⓓ the story does not say

3. Think about how the word *dog* relates to the word *barks*. What words relate in the same way?

   dog : barks

   - ⓐ rain : water
   - ⓑ cross : river
   - ⓒ buffalo : bow
   - ⓓ horse : neighs

4. Sitting Bull struggled across the river. What does *struggled* mean?
   - ⓐ to get in the water, to swim
   - ⓑ to talk gently, to not give up
   - ⓒ to fight hard, to try very hard
   - ⓓ to hunt buffalo, to use a bow and arrow

5. What answer lists in the right order what Sitting Bull did in his life?
   - ⓐ killed first buffalo, swept downstream, born in 1831
   - ⓑ born in 1831, swept downstream, killed first buffalo
   - ⓒ born in 1831, killed first buffalo, went to a neighing horse
   - ⓓ went to a neighing horse, stepped into swollen river, born in 1831

Arrested for Voting

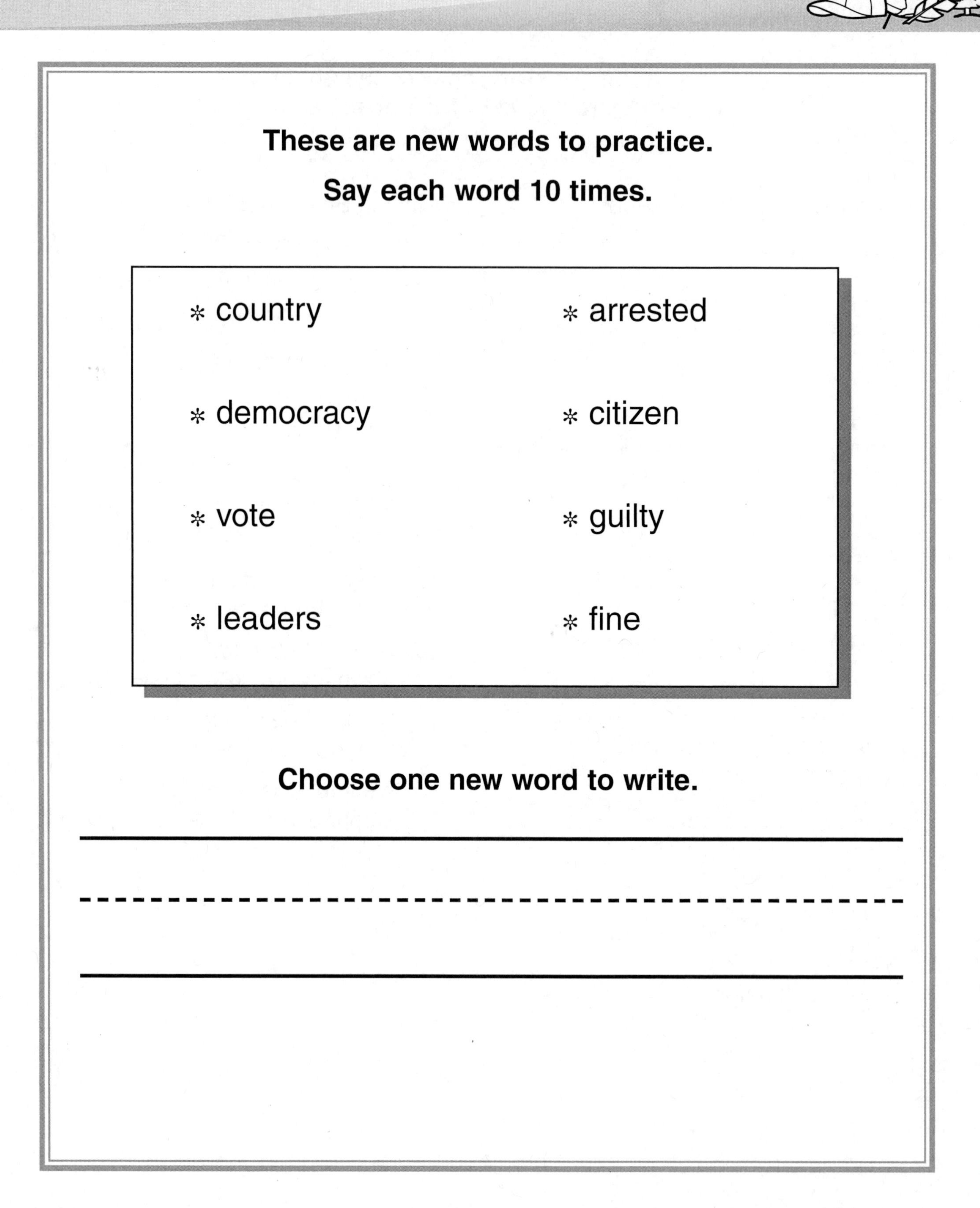

These are new words to practice.

Say each word 10 times.

- * country
- * arrested
- * democracy
- * citizen
- * vote
- * guilty
- * leaders
- * fine

Choose one new word to write.

Arrested for Voting

We live in a free country. Our country is a democracy. In a democracy, we vote. We vote for our leaders. We vote for people who make laws. We vote for leaders who will make laws we like. One day a woman named Susan voted. Susan was arrested. She was arrested for voting. Why was Susan arrested?

Susan B. Anthony

Susan B. Anthony was born in 1820. At that time, women could not vote. Only men could vote. Susan was smart. She learned how to read and write by the age of three. She became a teacher. She helped her students learn. Susan wanted to do more. She wanted to help everyone. She wanted to help women vote.

Susan worked hard. She talked to many people. In 1872, she voted. She said she could vote because of two laws. One law was about who could be a citizen. A citizen is a member of a country. The law said that one way to become a citizen of the United States was to be born in the United States. Susan was born in the United States. The other law said all citizens could vote. It said that citizens of any color could vote. It said that citizens who had been slaves could vote.

Susan had to go to court. The court would tell Susan if she was wrong to vote. The judge was angry. He did not let Susan talk! He said she was guilty. When you are guilty, you have done something wrong. He said Susan was guilty of breaking the law. She was guilty because she voted. He charged Susan a fine. A fine is money you have to pay.

Susan never paid the fine. She just worked harder. She talked to more people. Susan died in 1906. In 1920, a new law was passed. The law said women could vote. Susan's work helped pass this law. The law made our country a stronger democracy.

Arrested for Voting

After reading the story, answer the questions.
Fill in the circle next to the correct answer.

1. This story is mainly about
   - (a) voting
   - (b) democracy
   - (c) a new law
   - (d) Susan B. Anthony

2. What year did Susan vote?
   - (a) 1820
   - (b) 1872
   - (c) 1906
   - (d) 1920

3. A citizen is
   - (a) a democracy
   - (b) someone who can vote
   - (c) a member of a country
   - (d) someone who goes to court

4. Think about how the word *pay* relates to the word *fine*. What words relate in the same way?

   pay : fine

   - (a) see : look
   - (b) read : book
   - (c) judge : guilty
   - (d) vote : citizen

5. Why didn't Susan think she was guilty?
   - (a) because of what two laws said
   - (b) because she was not a citizen
   - (c) because Susan wanted to help everyone
   - (d) because the judge did not let her talk

All About Milk

These are new words to practice.

Say each word 10 times.

* milk	* udder
* important	* teat
* dairy	* produce
* attached	* healthy

Choose one new word to write.

All About Milk

Milk is important. It is one of the most important foods in the world. All around the world, people drink milk. They drink milk from cows. They drink milk from goats. They drink milk from water buffalo. They drink milk from reindeer. They drink milk from yaks. We eat food made from milk. Cheese is made from milk. Ice cream is made from milk. Yogurt is made from milk. Butter is made from milk.

At one time, all cows were milked by hand. It was hard work. A farmer could only milk six cows an hour. This was okay when you are a small farmer. This was okay when you only wanted milk for your family. Dairy farmers raise cows. They have hundreds of cows. They milk their cows two or three times a day. They cannot milk by hand. It would take too long. It would take too many workers.

Today, dairy farmers use milking machines. Milking machines were invented in 1894. With a milking machine, a dairy farmer can milk 100 cows an hour! Milking machines do not hurt the cows. The machines are attached to each cow's udder. A cow's udder is the baglike pouch on a cow's body. There are four teats on a cow's udder. The milk is pumped out of the teats with the attached machine.

Cows can make, or produce, a lot of milk. Some milk cows can produce over 100 glasses of milk a day! A farmer must take good care of his or her cows. A cow must be healthy to produce a lot of milk.

A farmer must give his or her cows lots of water. Cows need to drink two gallons (7.6 liters) of water for every one gallon (3.8 liters) of milk they produce! A farmer must give his or her cows lots of food. A healthy milking cow can eat up to 100 pounds (45 kilograms) of food a day!

All About Milk

After reading the story, answer the questions.
Fill in the circle next to the correct answer.

1. How many cows can a farmer milk by hand?

   ⓐ six cows in one day
   ⓑ 100 cows in one day
   ⓒ six cows in one hour
   ⓓ 100 cows in one hour

2. This story is mainly about

   ⓐ healthy cows
   ⓑ milk and cows
   ⓒ milking machines
   ⓓ where milk comes from

3. When you produce something, you

   ⓐ make it
   ⓑ drink it
   ⓒ invent it
   ⓓ attach it

4. There would not be large dairy farms if

   ⓐ the milking machine had not been invented
   ⓑ there were more goats, water buffalo, reindeer, and yaks
   ⓒ a farmer had to milk his or her cows more than once a day
   ⓓ a cow needed gallons (liters) of water and pounds (kilograms) food

5. Think about how the word *raise* relates to the word *grow*. What words relate in the same way?

   raise : grow

   ⓐ milk : cow
   ⓑ dairy : farm
   ⓒ drink : water
   ⓓ invent : make

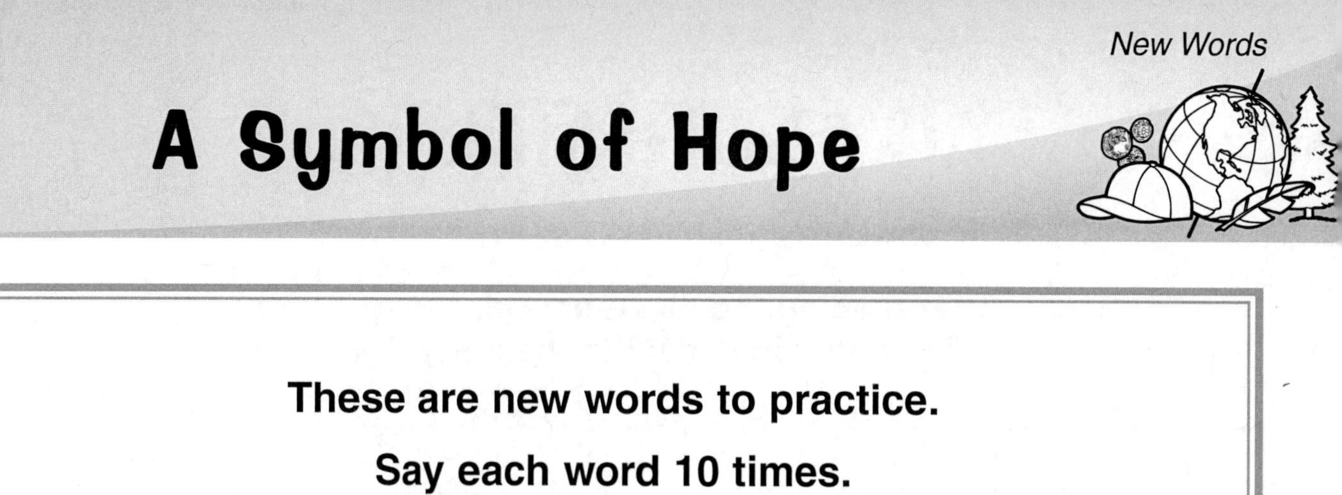

A Symbol of Hope

These are new words to practice.

Say each word 10 times.

* immigrants	* statue
* pedestal	* liberty
* torch	* symbol
* tablet	* huddled

Choose one new word to write.

A Symbol of Hope

"There she is!" All over the boat, people were pointing. They were crying, "There she is!" The people on the boat were immigrants. An immigrant is a person who goes to a new land. They go to make a new home. The immigrants were coming to the United States. They were coming to make a new home.

Who were the immigrants pointing at? Who were they looking at? The immigrants were looking at a lady. She was big. She was 150 feet (45 meters) tall. She was standing on a pedestal, or base. On her pedestal, she stood 302 feet (92 meters) high. She weighed 225 tons. One hand was raised. In it, she held a torch. In the other hand, she held a tablet. Written on the tablet was a date. The date was July 4, 1776. The date is Independence Day for the United States.

The lady with the torch and the tablet was a statue. She was the Statue of Liberty. To the immigrants, the Statue of Liberty was a symbol. She was a symbol of hope. She was a symbol of freedom. They felt as if she was greeting them.

The Statue of Liberty was a gift. She was a gift from France. Work on the statue began in 1875. She took over ten years to make. She was made in France. She was shipped to the United States. She could not be shipped in one piece. She was taken apart. She was put into 214 big boxes. She was put together again in New York.

A poem is written at the pedestal's entrance. It says, "Give me your tired, your poor / Your huddled masses yearning to breathe free." The immigrants were tired after their long trip. Many of them were poor. They had huddled or crowded together on the boat. They all had come for the same reasons. They had all come to be free.

A Symbol of Hope

After reading the story, answer the questions.
Fill in the circle next to the correct answer.

1. About how many years did it take to make the Statue of Liberty?
   - ⓐ 4
   - ⓑ 10
   - ⓒ 214
   - ⓓ 1875

2. Something that stands for another thing or idea is a
   - ⓐ torch
   - ⓑ statue
   - ⓒ tablet
   - ⓓ symbol

3. This story is mainly about
   - ⓐ a symbol of hope
   - ⓑ what the immigrants did
   - ⓒ a long, crowded boat ride
   - ⓓ how the Statue of Liberty was made

4. What might be one reason the Statue of Liberty was not shipped in one piece?
   - ⓐ It was so big.
   - ⓑ It was made in France.
   - ⓒ The boat was too crowded.
   - ⓓ The pedestal was made in the United States.

5. Think about how the word *pot* relates to the word *lid*. What words relate in the same way?

   pot : lid

   - ⓐ write : tablet
   - ⓑ statue : symbol
   - ⓒ immigrant : home
   - ⓓ pedestal : statue

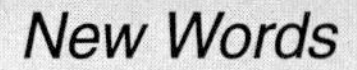

Saved from Rabies

These are new words to practice.

Say each word 10 times.

- attacked
- cure
- rabies
- microbes
- disease
- vaccine
- infected
- pasteurizing

Choose one new word to write.

Saved from Rabies

Joseph was nine years old. He was attacked. A dog attacked him. The dog bit him over a dozen times. The bites were deep. The dog had rabies. Rabies is a deadly disease. It is a deadly disease people can get from the bite of an infected animal. Joseph was bitten in 1885. At that time, there was no cure for rabies. People bitten by infected animals died.

Joseph's parents took him to a man. The man was Louis Pasteur. Pasteur was a scientist. He studied microbes. Microbes are tiny germs. Some microbes help us. Other microbes harm us. People did not know about microbes for a long time. Pasteur was one of the scientists who helped us learn. Pasteur studied how to protect people from deadly microbes.

Louis Pasteur

Pasteur wanted to protect people from rabies. He made a vaccine. A vaccine is used to fight disease. How does a vaccine work? The vaccine has microbes in it. The microbes are dead or very weak. There are not enough microbes to hurt you. But there are enough microbes for your body to learn how to fight the disease.

Pasteur did not want to use his vaccine on Joseph. Why not? Pasteur had not yet used his vaccine on people. He had only used his vaccine on dogs. Two doctors said Joseph was going to die. Only then did Pasteur say, "Yes."

Pasteur's vaccine worked. Joseph was saved! Pasteur had found a cure. Many other people were saved, too. Pasteur was born in France. Today, Pasteur's work is used not just in France. It is used all over the world. Pasteur taught us to heat our milk. By heating up our milk, we kill microbes in it. This is called pasteurizing. Do you see Pasteur's name in the word *pasteurizing*? Today, we pasteurize a lot of our foods.

Saved from Rabies

After reading the story, answer the questions.
Fill in the circle next to the correct answer.

1. How many doctors said Joseph was going to die?
   - ⓐ two
   - ⓑ nine
   - ⓒ twelve
   - ⓓ one hundred

2. This story is mainly about
   - ⓐ rabies
   - ⓑ Pasteur
   - ⓒ vaccines
   - ⓓ microbes

3. Why do we give vaccines?
   - ⓐ so we can learn about microbes
   - ⓑ so infected dogs will not bite us
   - ⓒ so we can kill microbes in our milk
   - ⓓ so our bodies can learn to fight diseases

4. If something is cured, it is
   - ⓐ infected
   - ⓑ a microbe
   - ⓒ made better
   - ⓓ pasteurized

5. Think about how the word *pasteurize* relates to the word *heat*. What words relate in the same way?

   pasteurize : heat

   - ⓐ dog : bite
   - ⓑ read : book
   - ⓒ freeze : cool
   - ⓓ microbe : germ

How Canada Got Its Name

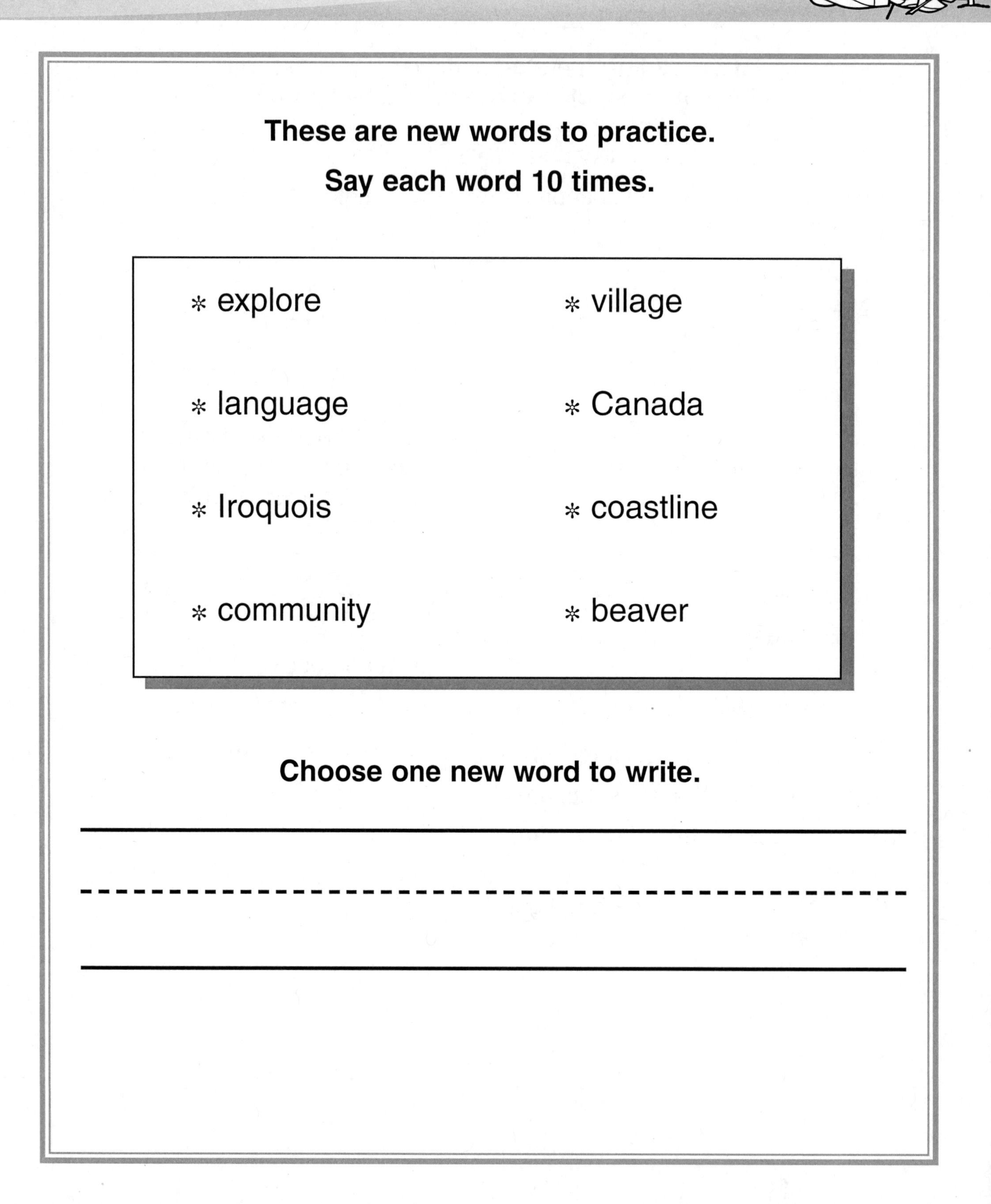

These are new words to practice.

Say each word 10 times.

- ✻ explore
- ✻ village
- ✻ language
- ✻ Canada
- ✻ Iroquois
- ✻ coastline
- ✻ community
- ✻ beaver

Choose one new word to write.

Story

How Canada Got Its Name

Jacques Cartier was an explorer. He was born long ago. He was born in 1491. He was born in France. He sailed in a boat. He sailed across an ocean. The ocean was the Atlantic Ocean. He wanted to explore new lands. He wanted to meet new people.

Cartier explored new lands. He saw new things. He met new people. The people did not speak French. They spoke their own language. They spoke Iroquois. *Kanata* is an Iroquois word. It means "community" or "village." A community is a group of people. The people live near each other. They work together. They share. They help each other. A village is small. It is smaller than a town. It is a small group of houses.

Jacques Cartier

Cartier heard the people say *kanata*. Cartier thought they were saying something else. He thought they were saying Canada. Cartier did not speak the Iroquois language. He did not know Iroquois words. He did not know the word *kanata*. He did not know it meant "community" or "village." He thought it was a name. He thought it was the name of the Iroquois land. He thought the name of the land was Canada!

Canada is big. It has lots of land. It is the second-largest country in the world. Only Russia is bigger. Three oceans touch Canada. The Atlantic Ocean touches it. The Pacific Ocean touches it. The Arctic Ocean touches it. Land that touches an ocean is called a coastline. Canada has a lot of coastline. It has more coastline than Russia. It has more coastline than any other country in the world!

Canada has lots of animals. One animal is the beaver. Lots of people came to Canada for the beaver. They were traders. They wanted furs. They set up trading posts. They traded for beaver furs. The furs were worth a lot. At one time they could even be used as money!

Quiz

How Canada Got Its Name

**After reading the story, answer the questions.
Fill in the circle next to the correct answer.**

1. What is a coastline?

   ⓐ an ocean
   ⓑ a community or village
   ⓒ land that touches an ocean
   ⓓ a country with lots of animals

2. What ocean did the explorer Cartier sail across?

   ⓐ Arctic
   ⓑ Pacific
   ⓒ Atlantic
   ⓓ Iroquois

3. This story is mainly about

   ⓐ an explorer
   ⓑ animals in Canada
   ⓒ the Iroquois language
   ⓓ Canada and how it got its name

4. What group of people would most likely make up a community?

   ⓐ people who ride bikes
   ⓑ people who sail in boats
   ⓒ people who have black hair
   ⓓ people who go to school together

5. Think about how the word *lake* relates to the word *ocean*. What words relate in the same way?

   lake : ocean

   ⓐ ocean : Arctic
   ⓑ village : town
   ⓒ Iroquois : land
   ⓓ language : beaver

Cattle Drive

These are new words to practice.

Say each word 10 times.

* herded	* abreast
* cattle	* stampede
* Texas	* lightening
* raised	* clockwise

Choose one new word to write.

Cattle Drive

Long ago, cowboys herded cattle. They drove them north. The cowboys started in Texas. The cattle were raised in Texas. Ranchers raised the cattle. We get beef from cattle. Lots of people wanted to eat beef. But some of those people were not in Texas. The people were in cities. The people were far away.

From 1866 to 1886, cowboys herded cattle. They herded more than six million! The cattle were driven to big railroad towns. There, the cattle were put on trains. The cattle were sent east. They were sent to where they were wanted. Some of the big railroad towns were in Kansas. One railroad town in Kansas was Dodge City.

Many herds had about 3,000 cattle. The cattle didn't move in a single line. They moved five or more abreast. When something is abreast, it is side by side. Cowboys rode in front. They rode in back. They rode on both sides. They kept the cattle moving. The cattle moved slowly. They went about 10 to 15 miles (16 to 24 kilometers) a day. They made a lot of dust. You could see the dust from miles away.

There was danger on the trail. The biggest danger was a stampede. A stampede is a sudden rush. It is a sudden flight. Storms often caused stampedes. A flash of lightening would scare the cattle. The flash of lightening would make the cattle stampede. Sometimes the cowboys would let the cattle run. The cattle would run until they were all tired out.

Other times, the cowboys would try to turn the cattle in front. They would try to make them turn a sharp right. If the cowboys could get the cattle in front to turn, the cattle behind would follow. All the cattle would turn to the right. They would all begin to move clockwise. Turning clockwise, the cattle would begin to circle in on each other. They would slow down. They would stop running away.

Cattle Drive

**After reading the story, answer the questions.
Fill in the circle next to the correct answer.**

1. This story is mainly about
   - (a) stampedes
   - (b) ranchers in Texas
   - (c) people who wanted beef
   - (d) cowboys and cattle drives

2. Where did the cattle drives start?
   - (a) Texas
   - (b) Kansas
   - (c) Dodge City
   - (d) Stampede City

3. When something turns clockwise, it turns
   - (a) to the east
   - (b) to the left
   - (c) to the north
   - (d) to the right

4. Think about how the word *front* relates to the word *back*. What words relate in the same way?

   front : back

   - (a) slow : fast
   - (b) drive : herd
   - (c) begin : start
   - (d) stampede : rush

5. Why did the cowboys drive the cattle?
   - (a) to keep them moving
   - (b) to make them walk abreast
   - (c) to get them to a railroad
   - (d) to stop them from stampeding

What the President Can't Do

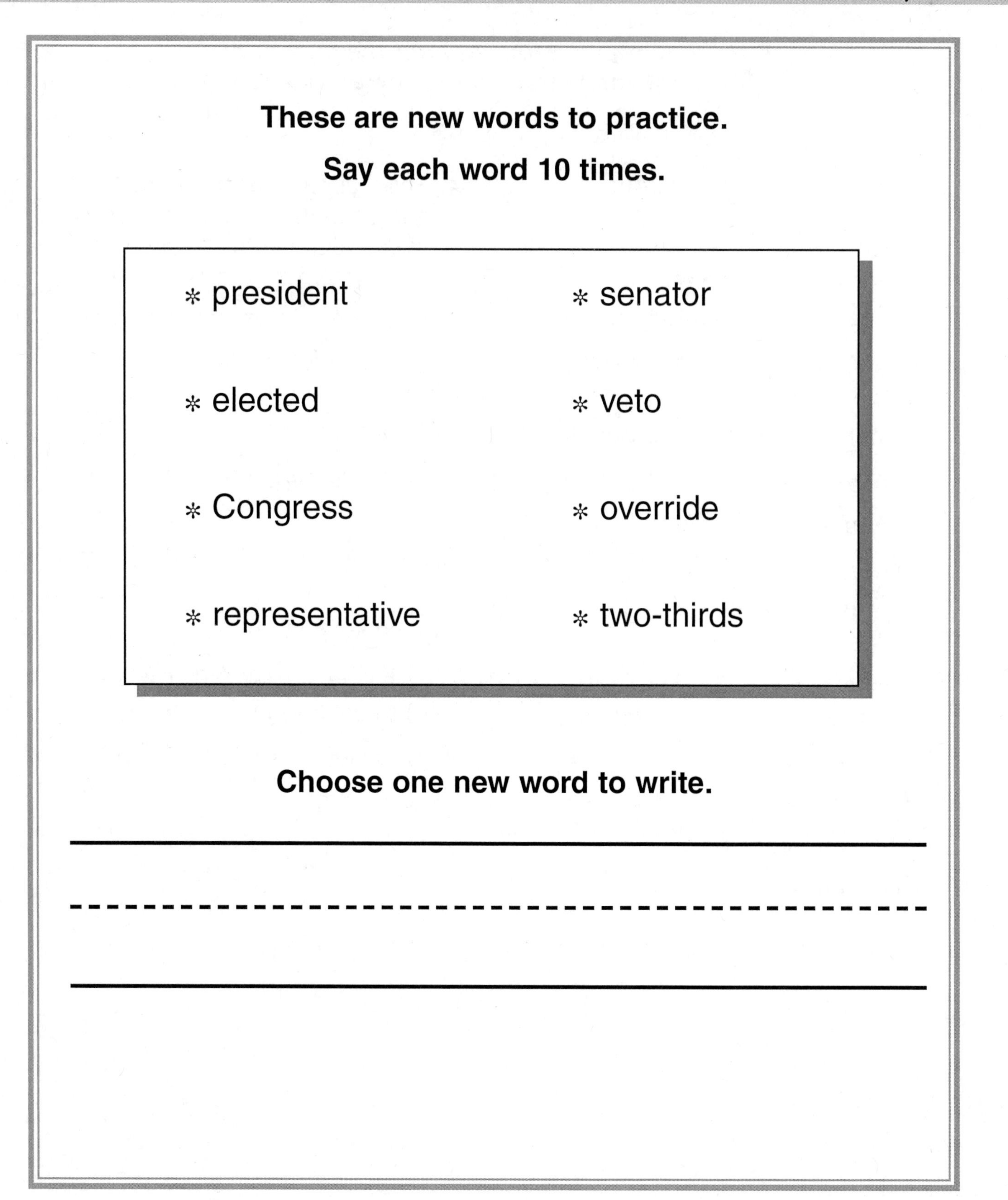

These are new words to practice.

Say each word 10 times.

- president
- senator
- elected
- veto
- Congress
- override
- representative
- two-thirds

Choose one new word to write.

What the President Can't Do

The president is a leader. In the United States, the president is elected. He or she is elected every four years. How is the president elected? People vote. They vote for a president every four years. The president leads the country. But there is one thing he or she can't do. What can't the president do?

The president can't make a new law. A law is a rule. The rules are to keep us safe. Some laws tell us what we can do. Other laws tell us what we can't do. We have laws about cars. We have laws about seatbelts. We have laws about schools. We have laws about food. We have laws about drugs.

A law starts with an idea. The idea may be new. The idea may be to change an old law. Only people in Congress can make a new law. Congress has two parts. One part is the Senate. One part is the House of Representatives. People in the Senate are called senators. People in the House are called representatives. Senators are elected. Representatives are elected. People vote for them.

First, someone in Congress writes a bill. Second, Congress votes on the bill. The House votes on the bill. The Senate votes on the bill. The bill must pass the Senate. It must pass the House. If it passes, the bill is sent to the president. The president can sign the bill. If the president signs the bill, the bill becomes a law.

The president may veto the bill. If a bill is vetoed, it is not signed. It does not become law unless something happens. Congress must override the veto. To override the veto, Congress must vote again. Two-thirds of both the House and Senate must vote to pass the bill again. If two-thirds vote for the new rule, the bill becomes a law.

What the President Can't Do

After reading the story, answer the questions.
Fill in the circle next to the correct answer.

1. What can't the president do?
   - ⓐ be a leader
   - ⓑ veto a bill
   - ⓒ make a new law
   - ⓓ get elected every four years

2. This story is mainly about
   - ⓐ the Senate
   - ⓑ how a law is made
   - ⓒ the House of Representatives
   - ⓓ how Congress can override a veto

3. The Senate is part of
   - ⓐ a bill
   - ⓑ Congress
   - ⓒ the president
   - ⓓ the House of Representatives

4. People do not elect
   - ⓐ bills
   - ⓑ senators
   - ⓒ presidents
   - ⓓ representatives

5. Think about how the word *law* relates to the word *rule*. What words relate in the same way?

   law : rule

   - ⓐ veto : bill
   - ⓑ House : senator
   - ⓒ idea : override
   - ⓓ president : leader

"Go for Broke"

These are new words to practice.

Say each word 10 times.

- * soldier
- * fought
- * Hawaii
- * Japan
- * plantation
- * Pearl Harbor
- * aid
- * senator

Choose one new word to write.

"Go for Broke"

Daniel K. Inouye can tie his shoes. He uses only his left hand. Why? Inouye lost his right arm. Inouye was a soldier. He fought in World War II. He was a brave soldier. He led a charge up a hill. He was shot, but still he would not stop fighting.

Inouye was born in Hawaii. He was born in 1924. His grandparents and father had come to Hawaii. They had come from Japan. Inouye's grandfather had come to work. His grandfather worked on Hawaii's sugar plantations. He worked twelve hours a day on the sugar plantations. He earned just ten dollars a month.

Inouye was in high school when Pearl Harbor was attacked. The attack took place on December 7th. The year was 1941. After the attack, the U.S. entered the war. When Pearl Harbor was attacked, Inouye saw the Japanese planes. He saw black smoke. He wanted to help. Inouye knew first aid. He had learned first aid because he wanted to become a doctor. Inouye worked hard taking care of hurt people.

Daniel K. Inouye

Later, Inouye signed up to be a soldier. He signed up for the 442nd Combat Team. The 442nd Combat Team was special. It was made up of Japanese-Americans. The men on the team were Americans. They were born in the U.S. Their parents had come from Japan to work. Inouye's combat team had a nickname. The nickname was "Go for Broke." "Go for Broke" meant that the men would never quit. The men would give everything they had. Inouye's team fought hard. They helped save many men.

After the war, Inouye never stopped "going for broke." He could not be a doctor with just one arm. But he could still fight! He could still defend Americans! He became a senator. He was the first Japanese-American senator in the U.S. In the Senate, he fought for all Americans. He fought for all Americans to be treated fairly.

"Go for Broke"

After reading the story, answer the questions.
Fill in the circle next to the correct answer.

1. Why couldn't Inouye become a doctor?
   - ⓐ He lost an arm.
   - ⓑ He knew first aid.
   - ⓒ He became a senator.
   - ⓓ He needed to work on Hawaii's sugar plantations.

2. Why does the nickname "Go for Broke" still fit Inouye?
   - ⓐ Inouye knew first aid.
   - ⓑ Inouye led a charge up a hill.
   - ⓒ Inouye worked taking care of hurt people.
   - ⓓ Inouye never stopped fighting for Americans.

3. This story is mainly about
   - ⓐ World War II
   - ⓑ a man who became a senator
   - ⓒ Hawaii's sugar plantations
   - ⓓ a combat team with the nickname "Go for Broke"

4. What statement is not true about Inouye?
   - ⓐ Inouye came from Japan.
   - ⓑ Inouye became a senator.
   - ⓒ Inouye fought in World War II.
   - ⓓ Inouye saw black smoke on December 7th, 1941.

5. Think about how the word *attack* relates to the word *fight*. What words relate in the same way?

   attack : fight

   - ⓐ quit : enter
   - ⓑ senator : Senate
   - ⓒ first aid : help
   - ⓓ sugar : plantation

Tomato Story

These are new words to practice.

Say each word 10 times.

* pizza	* Europe
* sauce	* Asia
* tomato	* Africa
* Italy	* cultivate

Choose one new word to write.

Tomato Story

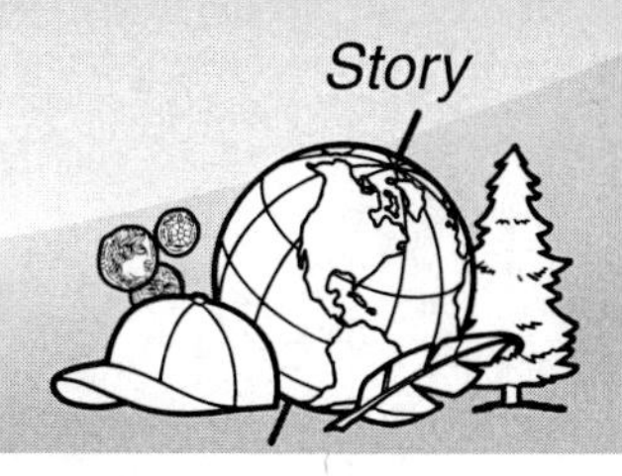

Think of pizza. We eat pizza. It has a crust. The crust is bread. The bread is on the bottom. On top of the crust is a sauce. The sauce is made out of tomatoes. It has spices in it. Cheese is on top of the sauce. The cheese is melted. Pizza was first made in Italy. It was made in the 1600s. It was brought to North America 300 years later. It was brought in the 1900s.

You can't have pizza without tomato sauce. You can't have tomato sauce without tomatoes. But where did tomatoes first come from? They did not come from Italy! Tomatoes were not in Europe. They were not in Asia. They were not in Africa. Tomatoes were only in the Americas! The tomatoes came from the Americas!

Tomatoes were first cultivated in Mexico. When you cultivate something, you grow it. You get the soil ready. You plant it. You take care of it. You weed it. You pick it. Where did the people in Mexico get the first seeds? They got them from tomato plants. The plants were wild. The wild plants grew in South America. These plants still grow in South America today.

Europeans first saw tomatoes in the 1500s. This was when they first landed in the Americas. The Europeans brought tomatoes back to Europe. At first, people did not eat tomatoes. They thought they were a bad food. They thought they made you sick.

The tomato is not a bad food. It does not make you sick. People in Europe learned this over time. Slowly, they began to eat tomatoes. They grew them. They ate more and more of them. By the 1800s, many sauces were made with tomatoes. Today, tomatoes are in Europe. They are in Asia. They are in Africa. They are grown all over the world. They are eaten all over the world. And, they are on pizza!

Tomato Story

After reading the story, answer the questions.
Fill in the circle next to the correct answer.

1. When did Europeans first see tomatoes?

   (a) in the 1500s
   (b) in the 1600s
   (c) in the 1800s
   (d) in the 1900s

2. What statement is true?

   (a) Eating tomatoes always makes you sick.
   (b) Today, tomatoes are eaten around the world.
   (c) Before the 1500s, tomatoes grew wild in Europe.
   (d) Most pizza is made with a sauce that does not have tomatoes.

3. This story is mainly about

   (a) food
   (b) tomatoes
   (c) how pizza uses tomatoes
   (d) how plants were first cultivated

4. Which happened first?

   (a) Pizza was brought to North America.
   (b) Sauces were made with tomatoes in Italy.
   (c) Tomato plants were cultivated in Mexico.
   (d) Tomatoes were brought from the Americas to Europe.

5. Think about how the word *top* relates to the word *bottom*. What words relate in the same way?

   top : bottom

   (a) tomato : food
   (b) pizza : crust
   (c) Italy : Mexico
   (d) wild : cultivated

The Oregon Trail

These are new words to practice.

Say each word 10 times.

* Oregon
* trail
* journey
* plains
* oxen
* dangerous
* roped
* guide

Choose one new word to write.

The Oregon Trail

A letter was written long ago. Someone who had gone over the Oregon Trail wrote it. The letter said, "Our journey across the Plains was a long and hard one. We lost everything but our lives."

The Oregon Trail was long. It was about 2,000 miles (3,220 kilometers) long. It started in Missouri. It ended in Oregon. It took about six months to cross. It was a journey filled with danger. There were flat, dry plains. Often, there wasn't enough water. One letter told about ground with "not a drop of water, not a spear of grass." It said there was "nothing but bare and broken rock, sand, and dust."

At other times, it was very cold. It snowed. Storms lasted for days. One letter said, "It has been raining all day long. The men and boys are soaking wet." People rode in covered wagons. They had to bring food. They had to bring tools. It all had to fit in the wagon. Oxen or horses pulled the wagons. The animals needed grass. It was hard to find grass for so many animals.

There were high mountains. The mountains were steep. Sometimes wagons had to be lowered down cliffs. Ropes were used. It was slow, hard work. There were rivers. Some rivers were big. The water was deep. It ran fast. It was dangerous to cross. Sometimes the wagons were roped together. Men on horses rode alone. They were not roped together. The men were river guides. They guided the oxen. They kept them heading in the right direction.

About 300,000 people went on this trail. Most went during the 1840s and 1850s. Why did so many people go? Why did they make this hard, dangerous journey? The people wanted to start a new life. They wanted land. The land at the end of the trail was free. It was good, rich land.

The Oregon Trail

After reading the story, answer the questions.
Fill in the circle next to the correct answer.

1. This story is mainly about
   - (a) danger
   - (b) letters
   - (c) starting a new life
   - (d) what the Oregon Trail was like
2. From the story, you can tell that
   - (a) oxen were as fast as horses
   - (b) the Oregon Trail was an easy journey
   - (c) people did not care about good, rich land
   - (d) letters can help us see what life was like long ago
3. Think about how the word *mountains* relates to the word *steep*. What words relate in the same way?

   mountains : steep

   - (a) plains : flat
   - (b) guide : river
   - (c) journey : trip
   - (d) letter : dangerous
4. What did people sometimes have to do in the mountains?
   - (a) rope the wagons together
   - (b) guide the oxen with horses
   - (c) lower the wagons with ropes
   - (d) bring tools to fit in the wagon
5. Where did the Oregon Trail start?
   - (a) Ohio
   - (b) Missouri
   - (c) Oklahoma
   - (d) Mississippi

The Man Who Didn't Wear Socks

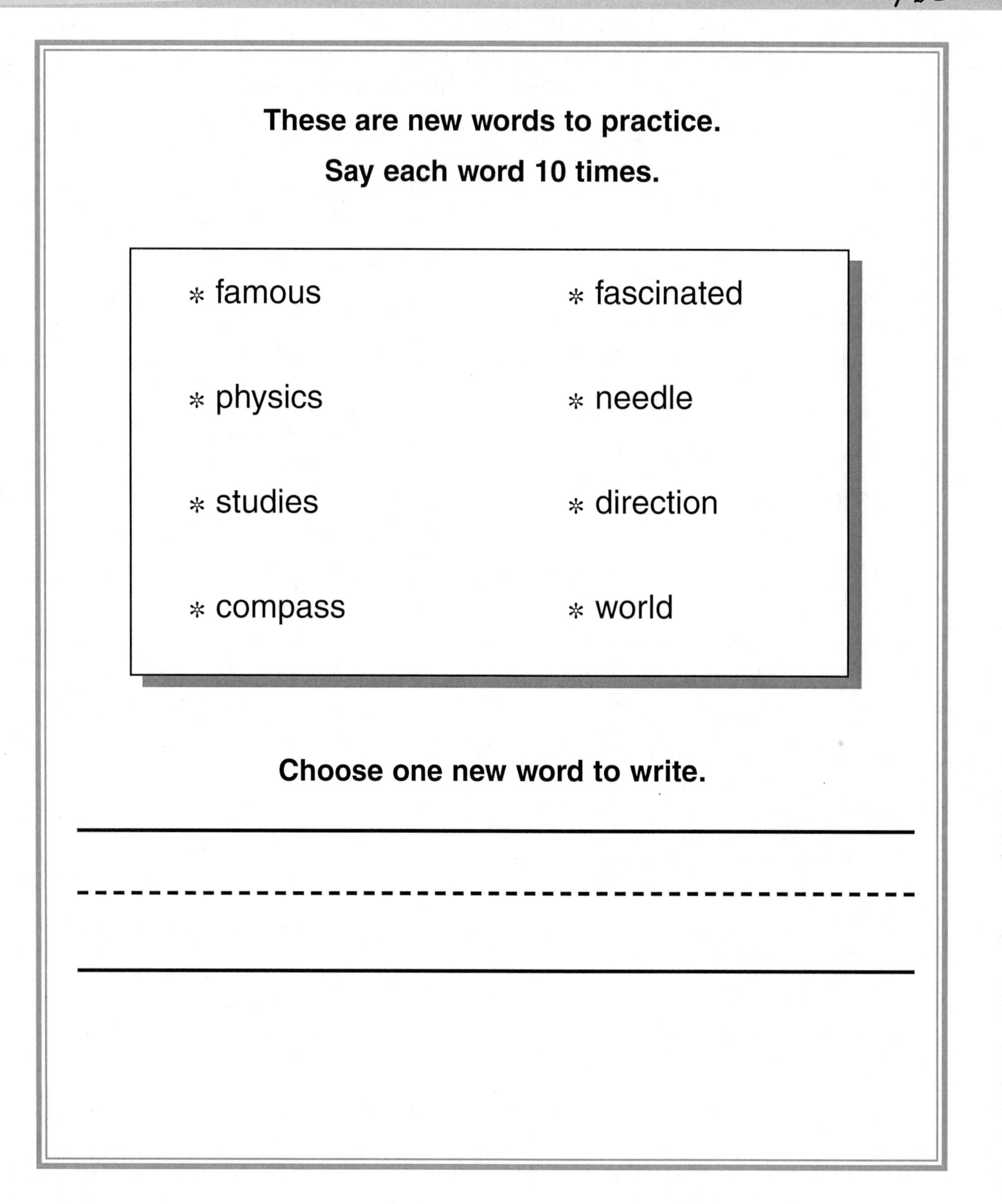

These are new words to practice.

Say each word 10 times.

- ✻ famous
- ✻ fascinated
- ✻ physics
- ✻ needle
- ✻ studies
- ✻ direction
- ✻ compass
- ✻ world

Choose one new word to write.

The Man Who Didn't Wear Socks

Albert Einstein is a famous scientist. He studied physics. Physics is a science. It deals with energy. It deals with matter. Matter is what things are made of. Matter is anything that takes up space. Physics studies the ways that things are moved. It studies how work is done.

Albert Einstein

Einstein was born in 1879. He was born in Germany. When he was five, he was sick in bed. His father gave him a compass. Einstein was fascinated. When you are fascinated by something, you are very interested in it. Einstein held the compass up. He held it down. He turned it left. He turned it right. The compass needle always pointed in the same direction. This made Einstein curious. Why did the needle always point in the same direction? Einstein kept thinking up more questions. Then, he would think up answers.

Some teachers did not think Einstein was smart. No one thought he would be famous. Why not? He was quiet. He was slow to speak. Often, he just stared into space. But Einstein was smart. He was just busy thinking. He was busy thinking up new questions and answers. Some of Einstein's questions and answers changed the way we think about our world.

Einstein left Germany. He left in 1933. Einstein was Jewish. At that time, Germany was not a safe place for Jews. Albert moved to the United States. People came from all over the world to talk to him. He was sent many letters. He was asked many questions.

Einstein did not wear socks. Why not? He found that the big toe always ended up making a hole in the sock. That is why he stopped wearing socks. Albert was asked what the most important thing to do in life is. "Never stop questioning," he said. "Never lose curiosity." And Einstein never did!

The Man Who Didn't Wear Socks

After reading the story, answer the questions.
Fill in the circle next to the correct answer.

1. When did Einstein leave Germany?
   - ⓐ 1879
   - ⓑ 1933
   - ⓒ when he was five
   - ⓓ when he stopped wearing socks

2. This story is mainly about
   - ⓐ a compass
   - ⓑ not wearing socks
   - ⓒ a famous scientist
   - ⓓ questions and answers

3. Sam loves physics. Sam is interested in how things move. Sam is __________ by physics.
   - ⓐ famous
   - ⓑ stopped
   - ⓒ curious
   - ⓓ fascinated

4. What lesson can be learned from Einstein?
   - ⓐ You should never wear socks.
   - ⓑ You should not ask teachers questions.
   - ⓒ You can be smart even if people don't think so.
   - ⓓ People are smart in different ways

5. Think about how the word *finger* relates to the word *hand*. What words relate in the same way?

   finger : hand

   - ⓐ toe : foot
   - ⓑ sock : hole
   - ⓒ question : answer
   - ⓓ compass : direction

The Underground Railroad

These are new words to practice.

Say each word 10 times.

- * underground
- * railroad
- * slavery
- * allowed
- * network
- * stations
- * passengers
- * conductors

Choose one new word to write.

The Underground Railroad

The Underground Railroad was not a real railroad. It was not for trains. It was not under the ground. What was it? Long ago, slavery was allowed in the United States. It was allowed in the South. Slavery is when one person owns another person. Slaves were brought from Africa. They were sold to different people. They were forced to work. They had to do what their owners said.

Slavery is wrong. You cannot own a person. Many people knew slavery was wrong. They wanted to free the slaves. You could not own slaves in the North. Slavery was not allowed. Some slaves tried to run away. They wanted to go north to Canada. They wanted to be free. They wanted to go where slavery was not allowed.

The Underground Railroad was a network of people. The people helped runaway slaves. Safe houses were called stations. Passengers were runaway slaves. Conductors were leaders. Conductors led slaves to where they could be free. They led their passengers to different stations. They led their passengers from safe house to safe house. They were in danger all the time.

Harriet Tubman was a famous conductor. Tubman was born a slave. When she was 28, she found out she was going to be sold. She ran away that night. She went by herself. She walked to freedom. It was a long, hard trip. She was in danger all the time. Tubman went back to the South 19 times. She led more than 300 slaves to freedom. Slave owners offered large rewards for her capture. Still, Tubman would not stop.

On one trip, Tubman was dressed like an old woman. She saw her old owner. She began to chase a chicken. Her old owner laughed. He thought the old woman was silly. He did not know it was Tubman! He did not know it was the woman everyone wanted to capture!

The Underground Railroad

After reading the story, answer the questions.
Fill in the circle next to the correct answer.

1. This story is mainly about
   - ⓐ war
   - ⓑ trains
   - ⓒ the South
   - ⓓ freeing slaves

2. When Harriet Tubman led runaway slaves north to Canada, she was a __________ on the Underground Railroad.
   - ⓐ station
   - ⓑ passenger
   - ⓒ conductor
   - ⓓ safe house

3. Think about how the word *teacher* relates to the word *student*. What words relate in the same way?

   teacher : student

   - ⓐ train : slave
   - ⓑ north : south
   - ⓒ station : safe house
   - ⓓ conductor : passenger

4. Why would Harriet Tubman dress up like an old woman?
   - ⓐ so she could be captured
   - ⓑ so no one would know who she was
   - ⓒ so her passengers would not know who she was
   - ⓓ so she could look silly and make people laugh

5. How many times did Harriet Tubman go back to the south?
   - ⓐ 19
   - ⓑ 28
   - ⓒ 300
   - ⓓ 1,861

A Store Like No Other

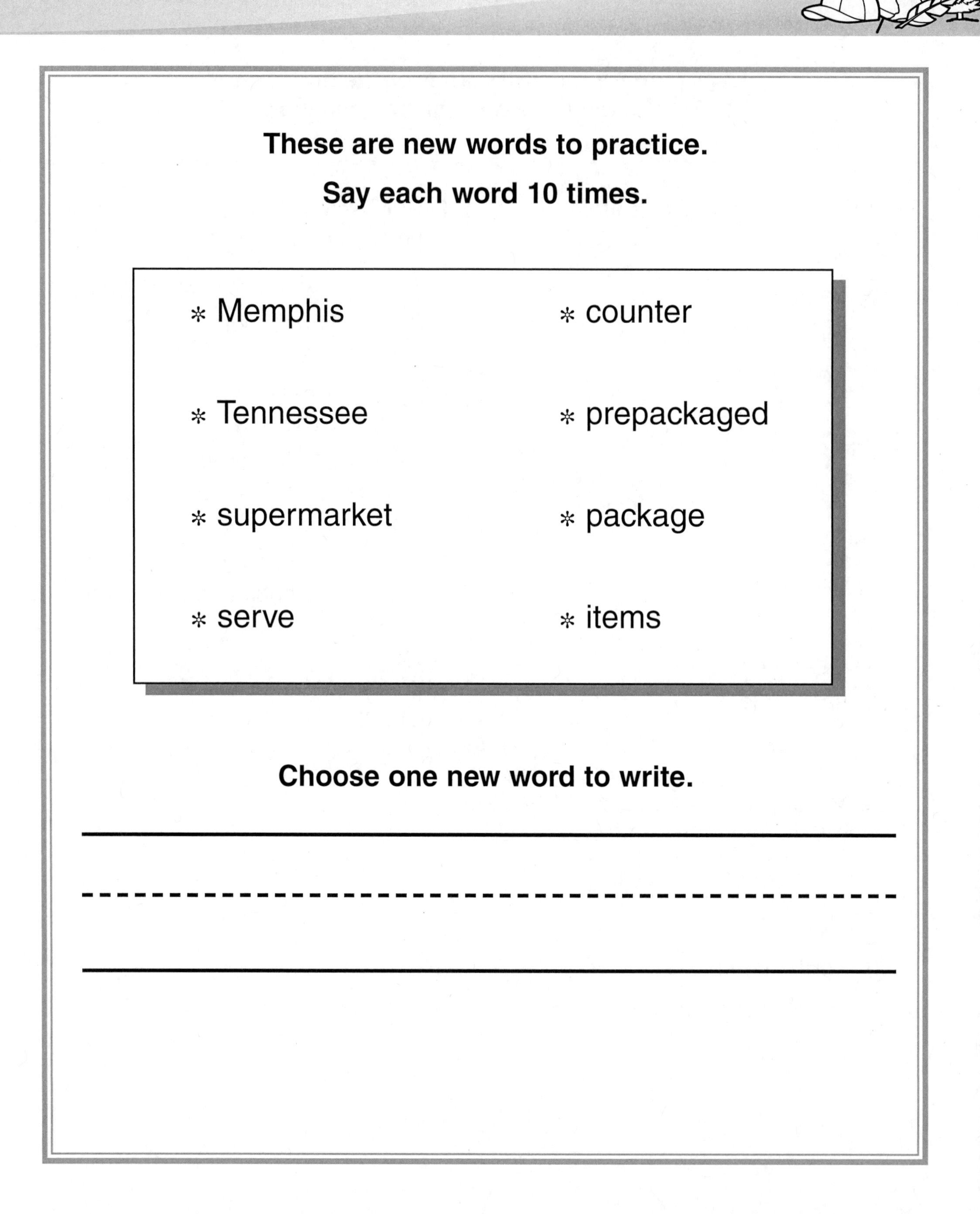

These are new words to practice.

Say each word 10 times.

- ✻ Memphis
- ✻ Tennessee
- ✻ supermarket
- ✻ serve
- ✻ counter
- ✻ prepackaged
- ✻ package
- ✻ items

Choose one new word to write.

A Store Like No Other

Earl said, “Grandma, I need your help. My teacher said I have to find out something. I have to find out something that is different. What is different from when you were a little girl? What is not the same?”

Earl’s Grandma said, “I grew up in Memphis. Memphis is a city. It is a city in Tennessee. In 1916 a store opened in Memphis. I had never seen a store like it. No one else had ever seen a store like it. There was no other store like it!”

Earl said, “What kind of store could it be? What kind of store had never been seen before?” The store was the first self-service store! It was the first supermarket! It sold food. But unlike other stores, you could serve yourself. You could get your own food. Before the store in Tennessee, you could not serve yourself. You had to wait in line. A person behind a counter helped you.

You would tell the person behind the counter what you wanted. The person would find it behind him or her. The person would get everything you needed. Nothing was prepackaged. Sugar and flour were in big bags. Other things were in big bags, too. They were not prepackaged. You would tell the person how much you wanted. Then, the person would measure out exactly how much you wanted. They would weigh it on a scale. They would package up what you wanted.

The store in Memphis changed everything. It changed the way we shop. Items were not behind a counter. You could serve yourself. The food was already packaged, or you could package it yourself. You could take your time thinking about what you wanted. Goods cost less, too. They cost less because storeowners did not have to pay so many people to help. Before, you could only choose from a couple of hundred items. Today, supermarkets have thousands of items!

A Store Like No Other

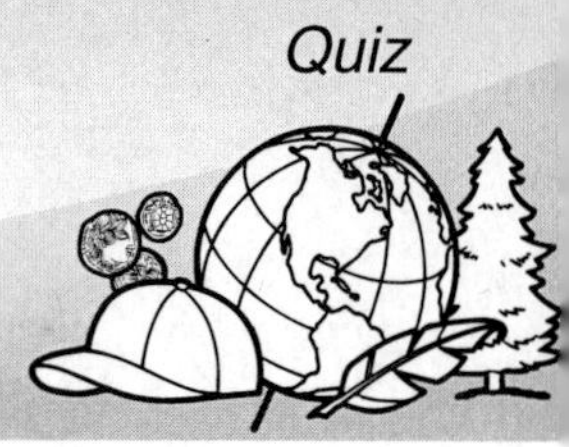

After reading the story, answer the questions.
Fill in the circle next to the correct answer.

1. This story is mainly about
   - ⓐ a different kind of store
   - ⓑ how things were not prepackaged
   - ⓒ Earl and what he had to find out
   - ⓓ what life was like for Earl's Grandma

2. When did the first self-service store open?
   - ⓐ 1716
   - ⓑ 1816
   - ⓒ 1916
   - ⓓ 2016

3. Think about how the word *see* relates to the word *look*. What words relate in the same way?

   see : look

   - ⓐ store : buy
   - ⓑ help : serve
   - ⓒ weigh : scale
   - ⓓ supermarket : thousands

4. Before the first self-service store, what did you do to get an item?
   - ⓐ You packaged it up yourself.
   - ⓑ You got it out of a big bag.
   - ⓒ You would measure out exactly how much you wanted.
   - ⓓ You told a person behind a counter what you wanted.

5. Why did goods cost less in the self-service stores?
   - ⓐ The items were prepackaged.
   - ⓑ There were thousands of items.
   - ⓒ You could take your time thinking about what you wanted.
   - ⓓ The storeowner did not have to pay as many people to help.

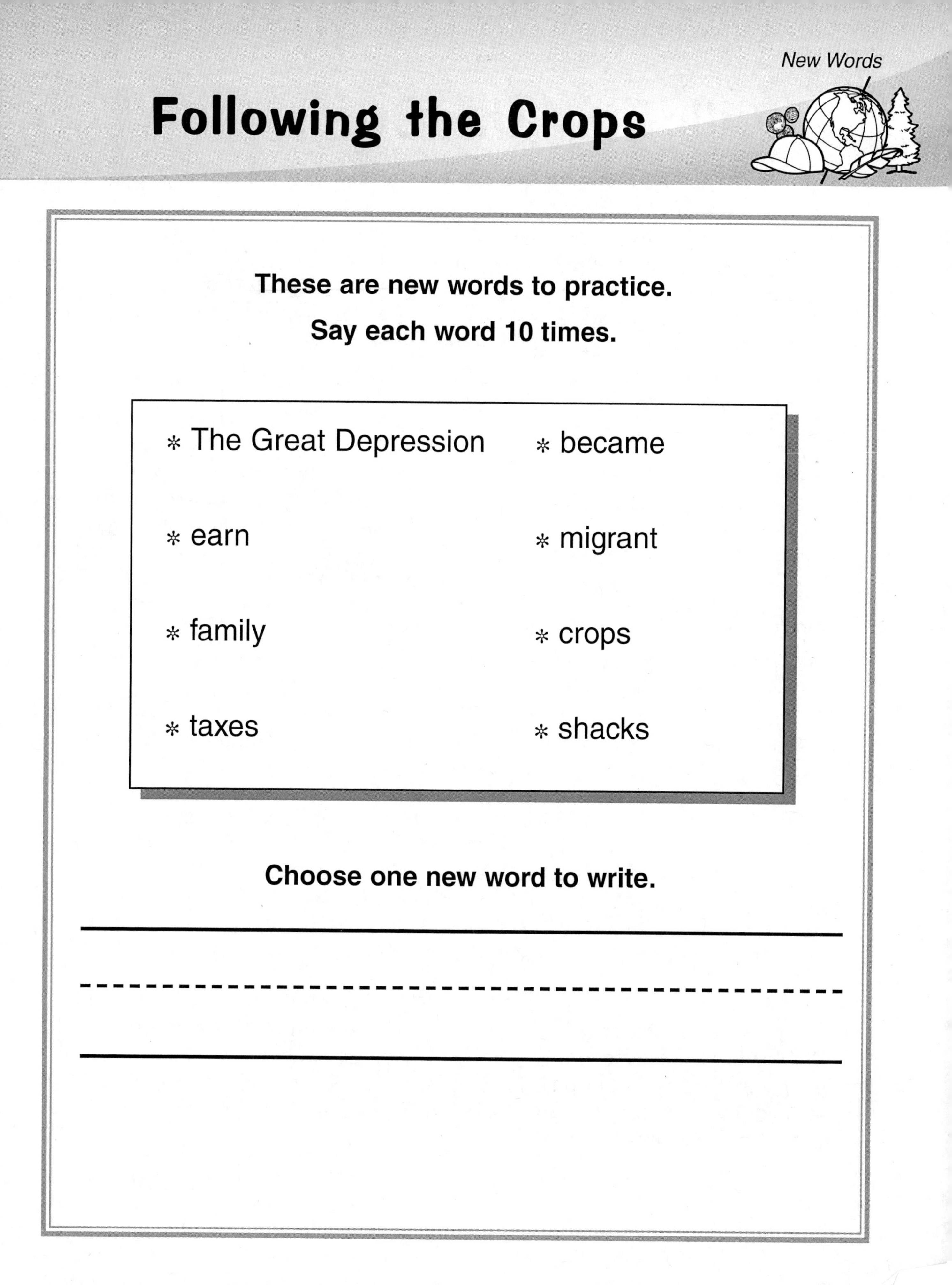

Following the Crops

These are new words to practice.

Say each word 10 times.

- * The Great Depression
- * became
- * earn
- * migrant
- * family
- * crops
- * taxes
- * shacks

Choose one new word to write.

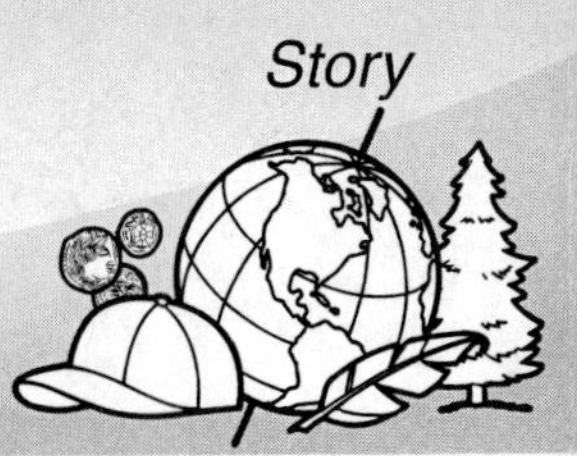

Following the Crops

César Chávez was born in 1927. He was born in Arizona. His father had a small store. His grandfather had a small farm. Everyone was happy. Then, the Great Depression came. The Great Depression started in 1929. All over the country, people lost their jobs. There was no work. People could not earn money. They lost their homes.

César Chávez

Chávez's father had to sell his store. The family had to move. They moved onto his grandfather's farm. They worked hard on the farm. But Chávez's family needed money. They needed money to pay taxes on the farm. Without money, they would lose the farm.

Chávez's father went to find work. He went to earn money to pay the farm taxes. He became a migrant farm worker. Migrant farm workers do not stay in one place. They move from farm to farm. They work for other farmers. They help plant crops. They help weed crops. They help pick crops. They work hard, but the jobs do not last long. They are paid very little.

Chávez's father worked hard. Still, he could not earn enough money to pay the taxes on the farm. So the family lost the farm. They had to go. They all became migrant farm workers. They had to live in shacks. The shacks did not have running water. The shacks did not have electricity. It was hard to go to school. Chávez could only go to a school for a few weeks. Then, his family had to move. They had to follow the crops. Over the years, Chávez went to over 30 schools!

One time Chávez's family picked grapes. They all worked hard. When the job was done, his family never got paid! There was nothing he and his family could do. Chávez knew this was wrong. When Chávez grew up, he worked to change things. He worked for better pay. He worked for better housing. He worked to help all migrant farm workers. He made a difference in the way migrant farm workers are treated today.

Following the Crops

After reading the story, answer the questions.
Fill in the circle next to the correct answer.

1. When did César Chávez become a migrant farm worker?

   ⓐ after they paid taxes
   ⓑ after they lost the farm
   ⓒ before his father sold his store
   ⓓ before he moved to his grandfather's farm

2. Why don't migrant farm workers stay in one place?

   ⓐ They live in shacks.
   ⓑ They are paid very little.
   ⓒ Their jobs don't last long.
   ⓓ They like going to lots of schools.

3. This story is mainly about

   ⓐ helping farmers
   ⓑ migrant farm workers
   ⓒ the Great Depression
   ⓓ César Chávez and his family

4. What is one reason a farmer might use migrant farm workers?

   ⓐ A farmer wants to work hard.
   ⓑ A farmer does not want to work hard.
   ⓒ When a crop is ripe, it needs to be picked quickly.
   ⓓ When a crop is ripe, it can wait to be picked.

5. Think about how the word *buy* relates to the word *sell*. What words relate in the same way?

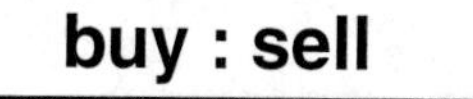

   ⓐ pay : taxes
   ⓑ move : stay
   ⓒ pick : crop
   ⓓ migrant : worker

Seward's Icebox

These are new words to practice.

Say each word 10 times.

* folly	* treaty
* icebox	* agreement
* Alaska	* nation
* Russia	* pipeline

Choose one new word to write.

Seward's Icebox

"Do not buy it!" "It is a waste!" "We do not want it!" "No to 'Seward's Folly'!" "No to 'Seward's Icebox'!" What did people mean? What didn't they want? What was a waste? What was "Seward's Folly"? What was "Seward's Icebox"?

Long ago, Alaska was not part of the United States. It was part of Russia. The United States signed a treaty. A treaty is an agreement. It is an agreement between nations. The treaty was with Russia. The treaty said there would be a sale. Russia would sell something. It would sell Alaska. The United States would buy it. The treaty was signed in 1867.

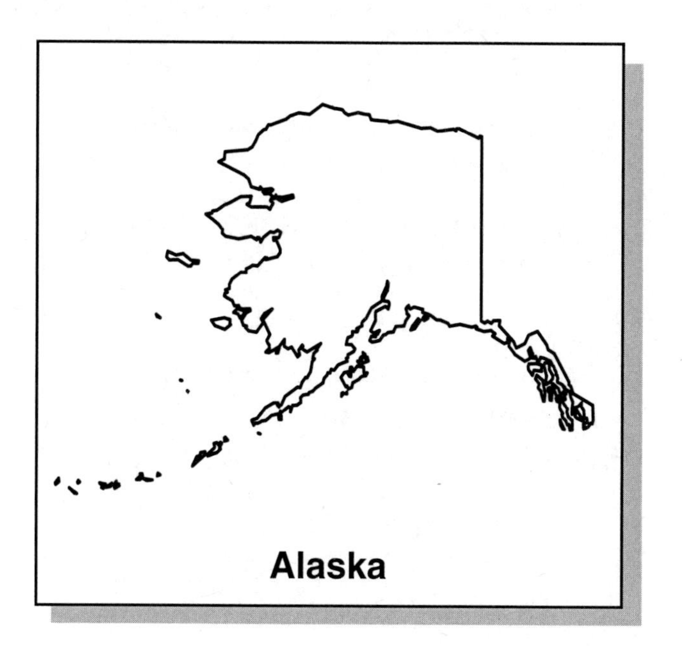

Many people did not like the treaty. They did not want Alaska. They did not want to buy it. "It is a waste," they said. "It is only ice! We do not want it. Do not buy it!" A man named Seward did not agree. He wanted the United States to be big. He wanted it to have lots of land. He wanted Alaska.

Some people called Alaska names. They called it "Seward's Folly." A folly is a foolish act. They thought it was foolish to buy Alaska. They called it "Seward's Icebox." They thought Alaska was cold. They thought it only had ice. People made fun of Seward. Still, Seward would not stop. He wanted land. He worked hard. He got the sale. He got Alaska.

The sale made the nation bigger. It added land. It added 570,374 square miles (1,477,269 hectares). What did it cost? It cost $7.2 million dollars. This was about two cents an acre (.4 hectares)! Was buying Alaska a folly? Was it foolish? Was it silly? Think about this: Alaska has fish. It has timber. It has oil. A pipeline was built. It was for oil. Oil was pumped through the pipeline. The first shipment was pumped on July 28, 1977. What was the one shipment worth? $7.2 million dollars!

Seward's Icebox

After reading the story, answer the questions.
Fill in the circle next to the correct answer.

1. What was the first shipment of oil worth?
   - (a) less dollars than what Alaska cost
   - (b) more dollars than what Alaska cost
   - (c) millions of dollars more than what Alaska cost
   - (d) the same number of dollars as what Alaska cost

2. This story is mainly about
   - (a) Russia
   - (b) buying Alaska
   - (c) names people called Alaska
   - (d) a treaty and the United States

3. A treaty is
   - (a) a waste
   - (b) a foolish act
   - (c) a pipeline built for oil
   - (d) an agreement between nations

4. Why did people call Alaska "Seward's Folly" and "Seward's Icebox"?
   - (a) They wanted to buy Alaska.
   - (b) They thought buying Alaska was a waste.
   - (c) They wanted to sign a treaty with Russia.
   - (d) They thought Alaska had lots of fish, timber, and oil.

5. Think about how the word *smart* relates to the word *wise*. What words relate in the same way?

   smart : wise

   - (a) buy : sell
   - (b) treaty : sign
   - (c) silly : foolish
   - (d) agreement : nation

Making Congress Fair

These are new words to practice.

Say each word 10 times.

* congress	* Senate
* United States	* Representatives
* Great Britain	* senators
* government	* census

Choose one new word to write.

Making Congress Fair

Many of our words come from old words. The word *congress* comes from old Latin words. The words mean "to come together." Long ago, the United States was not its own country. It was ruled by Great Britain. People united. They came together. They did not want to be ruled by Great Britain. They wanted to be free. The people went to war. They became free. They finally had their own country.

The people made a new government. The new government had a Congress. Congress makes laws. Congress has two parts. One part is the Senate. One part is the House of Representatives. Senators are in the Senate. Representatives are in the House. Members of Congress are elected. People vote for them.

The United States is made up of states. Today, we have 50 states. Some states are big. Others are small. Some states have a lot of people. Others have just a few. Big and little states have different needs. States with a lot of people have different needs than states with a lot fewer people. How can Congress be fair to all states? How can it be fair to all people?

Each state elects two senators. Big states elect two. Little states elect two. Today, we have 100 senators. Each one serves for six years. The senators make it fair for big and little states. There are 435 representatives. Every state elects at least one. Seven states elect just one. Alaska has one. Vermont has one. Other states elect more. In 2004, California had 53 representatives! New York had 29. Texas had 32.

How do we know how many representatives a state should have? Congress takes a census. A census is a count. People are counted. There is a census every ten years. It is the law. States with the most people get the most representatives. This makes it fair for states with a lot of people.

Making Congress Fair

After reading the story, answer the questions.
Fill in the circle next to the correct answer.

1. This story is mainly about
   - ⓐ new government
   - ⓑ the United States
   - ⓒ how Congress was made to be fair
   - ⓓ how senators and representatives are elected

2. When you come together, you are
   - ⓐ ruled
   - ⓑ united
   - ⓒ elected
   - ⓓ counted

3. If two different states each have 20 representatives, you know that
   - ⓐ both states have 20 senators
   - ⓑ the states are Alaska and Texas
   - ⓒ all the states have 20 representatives
   - ⓓ both states have about the same number of people

4. Think about how the word *representative* relates to the word *House*. What words relate in the same way?

   representative : House

   - ⓐ states : war
   - ⓑ senator : Senate
   - ⓒ government : Congress
   - ⓓ United States : Great Britain

5. Congress takes a census every ___ years.
   - ⓐ 10
   - ⓑ 30
   - ⓒ 52
   - ⓓ 435

Medical Detective

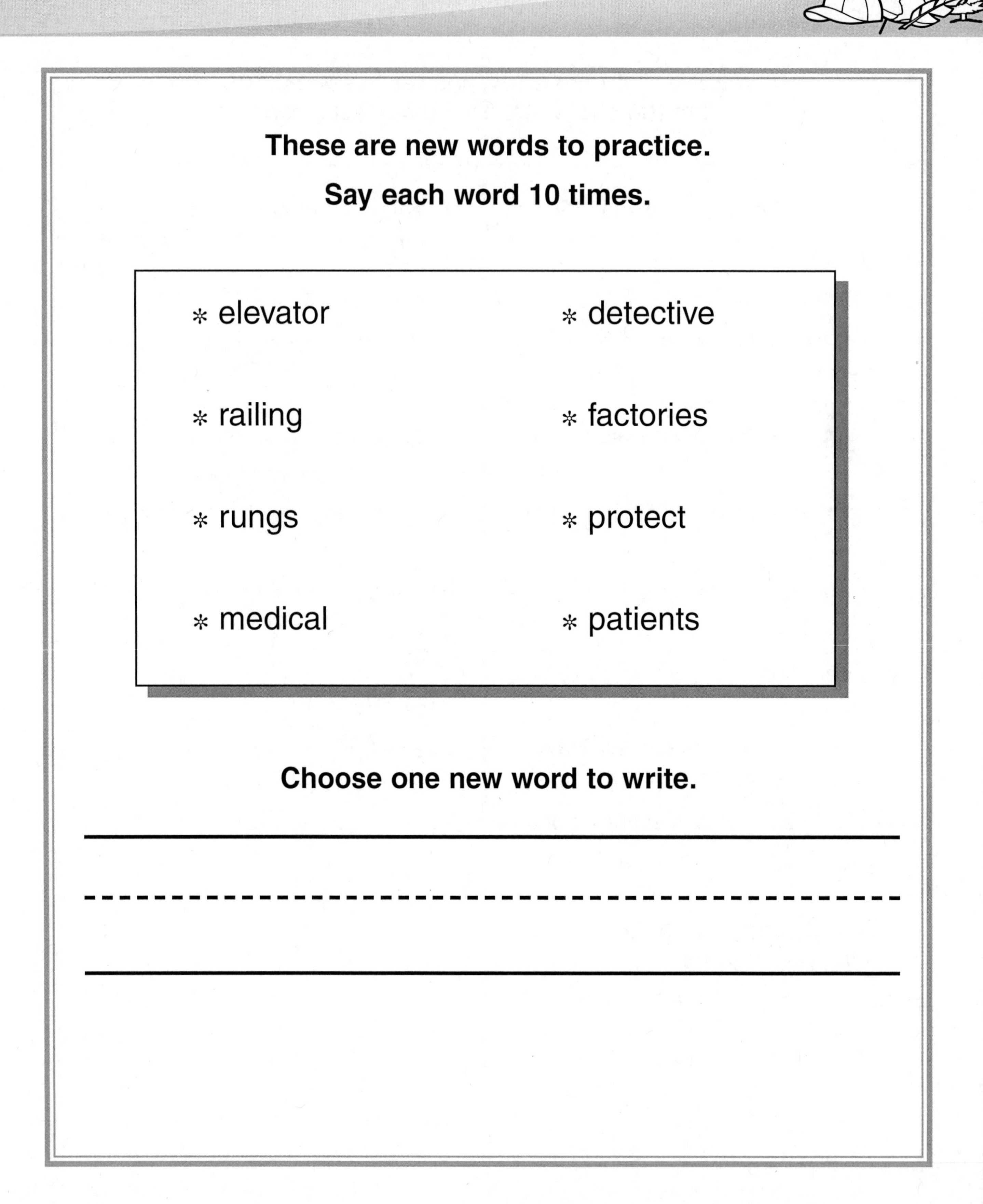

These are new words to practice.

Say each word 10 times.

- ✱ elevator
- ✱ detective
- ✱ railing
- ✱ factories
- ✱ rungs
- ✱ protect
- ✱ medical
- ✱ patients

Choose one new word to write.

Medical Detective

One day Alice Hamilton went into a mine. Hamilton stepped onto an elevator. The elevator didn't have any walls. Hamilton had nothing to hold on to. The elevator went down, deep into the black hole. It went down 800 feet (244 meters). Then, Hamilton crawled on her hands and knees. Next, she used an 80-foot (24 meters) ladder to climb down into a deep pit.

Alice Hamilton

Hamilton then crawled across another pit. She crawled across a high railing. The rungs on the railing were far apart. The rungs were so far apart that Hamilton had to stretch to reach them. Hamilton had to stay calm. She could not think about falling down into the pit.

Hamilton was not a miner. She was a doctor. What was she doing in the mine? Hamilton was a medical detective. Detectives try to find things. Hamilton tried to find out what jobs made people sick. The miners were getting sick. They did not know why. Hamilton went into the mine to find out. She looked at the men at work. She looked at their tools. She looked at what they were doing. She thought dust was making the miners sick.

Hamilton was born in 1869. Many factories were built at this time. Lots of people were hired to work in the factories. At that time, no one worried about the workers. There were no laws to protect them. Hamilton saw many poor patients. The patients worked in the factories. The patients were all very ill.

Hamilton asked her patients lots of questions. She would visit their homes. She would go to their work. She would find out what made them sick. She worked very hard to make the factories safer. She wanted to protect her patients. She taught other doctors how to be medical detectives. She worked for laws to be made. Today, we have laws about work. We have laws about factories. The laws help keep our workers safe.

Quiz

Medical Detective

After reading the story, answer the questions.
Fill in the circle next to the correct answer.

1. What did Alice Hamilton think was making the miners sick?

   ⓐ dust
   ⓑ factories
   ⓒ their tools
   ⓓ what they were doing

2. This story is mainly about

   ⓐ a mine
   ⓑ a doctor
   ⓒ factories
   ⓓ laws to protect workers

3. If Alice Hamilton saw a sick patient she would

   ⓐ make a law
   ⓑ think about falling into a pit
   ⓒ teach other doctors to be medical detectives
   ⓓ work hard to find out what made him or her sick

4. When you climb across a railing or up and down a ladder, you step on

   ⓐ pits
   ⓑ tools
   ⓒ rungs
   ⓓ elevators

5. Think about how the word *teacher* relates to the word *student*. What words relate in the same way?

   teacher : student

   ⓐ miner : mine
   ⓑ worker : factory
   ⓒ doctor : patient
   ⓓ detective : medical

What the Shoes Told

These are new words to practice.

Say each word 10 times.

* shoes	* popular
* pointed	* stuffed
* curled	* whalebone
* poked	* measured

Choose one new word to write.

What the Shoes Told

A man sat down to eat. He sat at a table. It was the year 1310. He was wearing shoes. The shoes were made out of leather or velvet. The shoes were long and pointed. The pointed tips curled at the end. The shoes were so long that the tips poked out all the way to the other side of the table! What do you know about this man? What do his shoes tell you?

The man was wearing shoes popular in the 1300s. When something is popular, it is well liked by many people. The shoes were popular in Europe. The toes of the shoes had to be stuffed because they were so long. The toes were stuffed with hay, wool, or moss. They were shaped with whalebone. The whalebone kept the curled tips pointing up.

Think about how long the man's shoes were. They were so long that the tips poked out all the way to the other side of the table. Do you think it would be easy or hard to walk in shoes that long? It would be very hard to walk in long shoes. You would have to take careful steps. It would be hard not to fall on your face.

From the man's shoes, you can tell that he was rich. A rich man would not need to work or walk much. So, he could wear shoes that were hard to walk in. One king made rules about shoes. Edward III was the king of England. He lived from 1322 to 1377. The king said he was the only one who could wear shoes as long as he wanted.

The king said that everyone else had to measure his shoes. Noblemen could not have tips that measured longer than 24 inches (60 centimeters). Gentlemen could not have tips that measured longer than twelve inches (30 centimeters). Common men could not have tips that measured longer than six inches (15 centimeters).

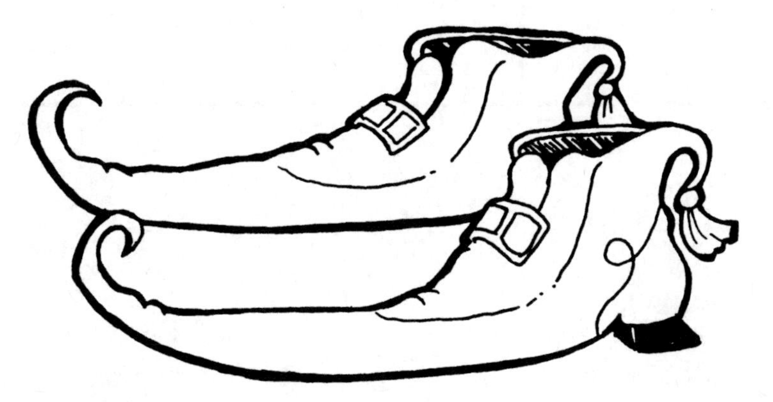

Quiz

What the Shoes Told

After reading the story, answer the questions.
Fill in the circle next to the correct answer.

1. This story is mainly about
   - ⓐ rules about shoes
   - ⓑ how shoes are made
   - ⓒ rich men in the 1300s
   - ⓓ a kind of shoe long ago

2. Many people like tennis shoes today. Tennis shoes are
   - ⓐ curled
   - ⓑ popular
   - ⓒ stuffed
   - ⓓ measured

3. Think about how the word *shoe* relates to the word *foot*. What words relate in the same way?

   shoe : foot

   - ⓐ hat : head
   - ⓑ sock : shoe
   - ⓒ leg : pants
   - ⓓ hand : mitten

4. What kept the curled tips of the shoes pointing up?
   - ⓐ moss
   - ⓑ wool
   - ⓒ leather
   - ⓓ whalebone

5. Why could a rich man wear shoes that were hard to walk in?
   - ⓐ A rich man could eat with the king.
   - ⓑ A rich man did not fall on his face.
   - ⓒ A rich man did not need to walk much.
   - ⓓ A rich man could not take careful steps.

Work Parties

These are new words to practice.

Say each word 10 times.

* proverb	* heavy
* families	* task
* axes	* quilts
* diary	* design

Choose one new word to write.

Work Parties

A proverb is an old saying. Often, proverbs say something wise. Early settlers had one old, wise saying. It went like this: *Many hands make light work*. Life was hard for early settlers. They had to work hard. But why work alone? If you have a work party, something hard becomes fun. After all, many hands make light work!

One work party was the chopping bee. Chopping bees were held for a man who had just gotten married. They were held for new families who had just arrived, too. Timber needed to be cut down so a house could be built. Land needed to be cleared so a garden could be planted.

Men would come early. Some of them would walk or ride for several hours to get there. They would bring their sharpest axes. They used their axes to chop down trees. One settler wrote about chopping bees in her diary. She wrote in her diary that a lot of land was cleared in a single bee. She said that 5 to 8 acres (2 to 3.2 hectares) of heavily timbered land was often cleared.

Settlers needed houses to live in. They needed barns for their animals. They had house raisings. They had barn raisings. These work parties began early in the morning. It was a big job, or task, to raise the heavy beams. The men could not do this task alone. They worked together to lift the heavy beams. After, families would eat together. They would play games.

Work parties were held to make quilts. These were called quilting bees. A quilt is like a blanket. It is made of two pieces of fabric. Padded material goes between the two fabric pieces. The pieces are stitched together. Some quilts had fancy designs. Other quilts were patched together in a hit-or-miss design. Women would talk and eat while they worked. One quilting bee in 1752 lasted for ten days!

Work Parties

After reading the story, answer the questions.
Fill in the circle next to the correct answer.

1. When might a chopping bee be held?
   - ⓐ when a barn needed to be raised
   - ⓑ when women wanted to make a quilt
   - ⓒ when a new family had just arrived
   - ⓓ when men needed to work together to raise heavy beams

2. This story is mainly about
   - ⓐ work parties
   - ⓑ working hard
   - ⓒ an old saying
   - ⓓ chopping bees

3. A task is a
   - ⓐ job
   - ⓑ beam
   - ⓒ design
   - ⓓ proverb

4. What does "Many hands make light work" mean?
   - ⓐ Some sayings are old and wise.
   - ⓑ Working together makes work fun.
   - ⓒ Many people need to lift heavy things.
   - ⓓ You don't work as hard if other people work.

5. Think about how the word *light* relates to the word *heavy*. What words relate in the same way?

   light : heavy

   - ⓐ chop : ax
   - ⓑ barn : raise
   - ⓒ tree : timber
   - ⓓ alone : together

The Rockies

These are new words to practice.

Say each word 10 times.

* backbone	* separates
* connected	* grizzlies
* ranges	* geysers
* The Continental Divide	* eruptions

Choose one new word to write.

The Rockies

You have a backbone. It is your spine. Your spine is a long row of bones. The bones run down your back. They are in the middle. They are all connected. The Rocky Mountains are the backbone of North America. The backbone is a chain. It is a chain of mountain ranges. Over 100 smaller mountain ranges make up the chain. The ranges are all connected. They run for over 3,000 miles (4,800 kilometers). They run from Alaska to New Mexico. They run north to south.

The Rockies form part of a line. The line is high. It is the Continental Divide. It is a line of the highest points in North America. The line divides the continent. Many rivers begin in the Rockies. They begin in the high peaks. The Continental Divide separates many rivers. It separates rivers that flow east from those that flow west.

Many animals live in the Rockies. Some animals are big. Grizzlies are big bears. They live in the northern Rockies. A big grizzly can eat up to 90 pounds (41 kilograms) of food a day! Grizzlies eat both meat and plants. They eat fish and insects. They eat berries, too. All mother bears are very good mothers. Baby bears are called cubs. Mother bears take good care of their cubs.

There are many hot spots in the Rockies. The hot spots are due to magma. Magma is hot liquid. The liquid is melted rock. Magma rises from far below the Earth's crust. It rises near the surface. It heats up water near the surface.

Hot springs are a type of hot spot. The water in the springs is hot. People bathe in some hot springs. Geysers are a type of hot spot. Geysers are eruptions. They are eruptions of steam and water. They erupt from cracks in the Earth's surface. They shoot steam and water. They shoot high into the air.

The Rockies

After reading the story, answer the questions.
Fill in the circle next to the correct answer.

1. This story is mainly about
   - (a) a chain of mountains
   - (b) the Continental Divide
   - (c) animals in the Rockies
   - (d) geysers and other hot spots

2. Magma is
   - (a) hot liquid rock
   - (b) a good mother bear
   - (c) a spring with hot water
   - (d) an eruption of steam and water

3. What is true of the Continental Divide?
   - (a) It is your spine.
   - (b) It is a type of hot spot.
   - (c) It rises from below the Earth's surface.
   - (d) It separates many rivers that flow east from those that flow west.

4. Think about how the word *smaller* relates to the word *bigger*. What words relate in the same way?

   smaller : bigger

   - (a) bear : cub
   - (b) spring : water
   - (c) mountain : peak
   - (d) connected : separated

5. Grizzlies live in the
   - (a) eastern Rockies
   - (b) western Rockies
   - (c) northern Rockies
   - (d) southern Rockies

Twelve People in a Box

These are new words to practice.

Say each word 10 times.

* jury
* juror
* accused
* trial
* charges
* lawyer
* judge
* decides

Choose one new word to write.

Twelve People in a Box

Twelve people sit in a box. The box is in a courtroom. The box is a jury box. The twelve people make up a jury. Each person is a juror. Mothers may be jurors. Fathers may be jurors. Teachers may be jurors. Doctors may be jurors. All kinds of people can be jurors.

If a person is accused of doing something wrong, he or she has the right to a trial. If you are accused of something, you are blamed. You are charged. Sometimes a trial is needed to see if the charges are correct. One side tries to prove that the charges are correct. The other side tries to prove that the charges are not correct. Each side has lawyers. Lawyers are people who know all about laws.

A trial takes place in court. Sometimes, a judge decides if the charges are correct. Other times, the lawyers ask the judge for a trial by jury. Everyone has the right to a trial by jury if they ask. In a trial by jury, the jury decides if the charges are correct.

Letters are sent to all kinds of people. The people do many different jobs. Some people are rich. Some people are poor. All the people are U.S. citizens. All the people are at least 18 years old. The letters tell the people to come to court. In court, lawyers talk to all the people. The jury is chosen.

The jury sits together. They sit in a jury box. They listen to all the lawyers. The judge listens, too. The judge makes sure that court rules are obeyed. The judge makes sure that the trial is fair. After the trial, the jury goes away. They go away to talk together. No one else is there. The jury decides. It decides if the charges are correct. Sometimes it takes only 30 minutes to decide. Sometimes it takes days or even weeks!

Quiz

Twelve People in a Box

**After reading the story, answer the questions.
Fill in the circle next to the correct answer.**

1. This story is mainly about
   - (a) what lawyers do in court
   - (b) what happens when someone is charged
   - (c) what a jury does and who makes it up
   - (d) what judges do when there is not a jury

2. Who could not be on a jury?
   - (a) someone who is poor
   - (b) someone who is a rich
   - (c) someone who is a U.S. citizen
   - (d) someone who is twelve years old

3. Think about how the word *juror* relates to the word *box.* What words relate in the same way?

   juror : box

   - (a) lawyer : side
   - (b) judge : decide
   - (c) teacher : desk
   - (d) mother : child

4. What happens first?
   - (a) A jury is chosen.
   - (b) A person is charged.
   - (c) Letters are sent out.
   - (d) Lawyers ask for a trial by jury.

5. If someone is accused, they
   - (a) are blamed
   - (b) sent a letter
   - (c) are chosen to be a juror
   - (d) decide if the charges are correct

True Stories About Money

These are new words to practice.

Say each word 10 times.

* bartered
* exchange
* item
* salt
* salary
* cocoa
* chocolate
* Central America

Choose one new word to write.

True Stories About Money

Long ago, people did not use money the way we do today. They bartered. When you barter, you pay for goods with other goods. You do not pay for goods with money. You trade. You exchange one item for another. If you were a farmer, perhaps you traded corn for cloth. Perhaps you traded oranges for fish.

Bartering can be hard. What if you did not want cloth? What if you did not want fish? To make trading easier, people began to use money. Instead of exchanging one item for another, you would exchange an item for money. Then, you could take your money and buy what you wanted.

Different things have been used as money. Stones have been used. Seashells have been used. Cows and sheep have been used. Even salt has been used as money! Long ago, Roman soldiers were paid in salt. When you work, you earn money. You earn a salary. A salary is what you get paid. Look at the words "salt" and "salary." The word "salary" comes from the Roman word "salt"!

Can you drink money? You cannot drink money today, but you could long ago. Once, cocoa beans were used as money. Chocolate is made from cocoa beans. The cocoa beans were grown in Central America. They were used as money in Central America. Rich people had lots of cocoa beans. They had so many that they could cook some beans. They would boil them in hot water. They would make a chocolate drink. They would drink their money!

Paper money is light. It is not heavy. It is easier to carry than a stone. It is easier to carry than a cow. Paper money was first made in China. An early name for China's paper money was "flying money." This was because it was easy for the money to blow away.

Quiz

True Stories About Money

After reading the story, answer the questions.
Fill in the circle next to the correct answer.

1. This story is mainly about

   (a) salt
   (b) goods
   (c) money
   (d) cocoa beans

2. When you work, you get paid

   (a) an item
   (b) a salary
   (c) an exchange
   (d) a cocoa bean

3. What can you make if you boil cocoa beans?

   (a) salt
   (b) money
   (c) flying money
   (d) a chocolate drink

4. Think about how the word *light* relates to the word *heavy*. What words relate in the same way?

   light : heavy

   (a) easy : hard
   (b) salt : salary
   (c) trade : exchange
   (d) cocoa beans : chocolate

5. Paper money could blow away. Why do you think people still used it?

   (a) It was light.
   (b) It was made in China.
   (c) It could be used for salt.
   (d) It could not be made into a drink.

Fighting Fire!

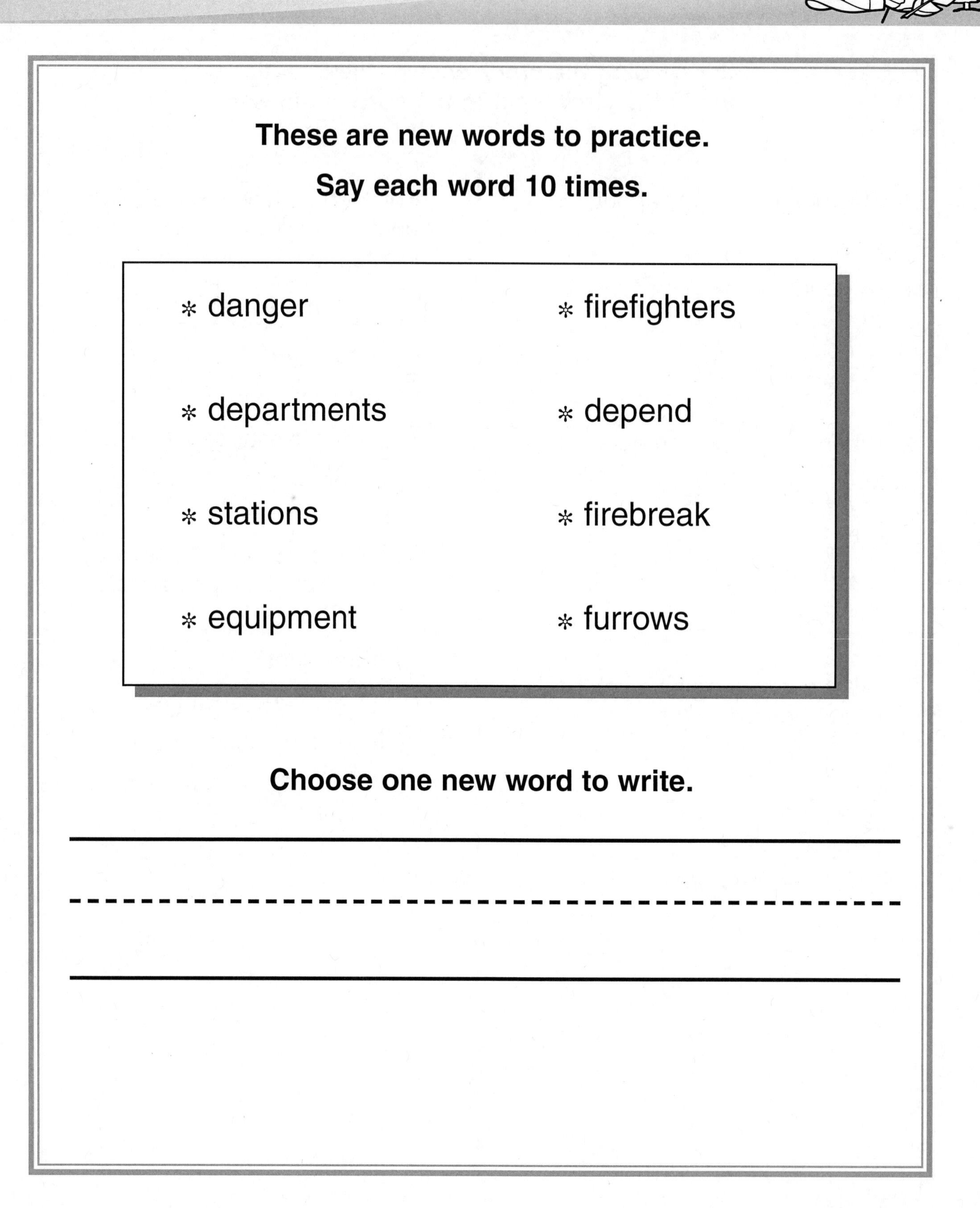

These are new words to practice.

Say each word 10 times.

- danger
- firefighters
- departments
- depend
- stations
- firebreak
- equipment
- furrows

Choose one new word to write.

Fighting Fire!

The early settlers faced many dangers. One danger was fire. Some fires started when people were careless. Lightening started other fires.

Today, we have fire departments. We have fire stations. We have fire trucks. We have special tools and equipment. What did people do long ago? What did they do before there were fire departments? What did they do without fire stations and trucks? What did they do when there were not any firefighters to fight fires?

Early settlers had to depend upon themselves. On the prairies, settlers could see a fire from far away. The smoke from it was like a great, huge cloud. It covered the earth. It blotted out the sun. As the fire got closer, the settlers could hear it roaring. They could see its red, rolling flames. They could see animals running fast in front of its rolling flames. The animals were running for their lives. It was hard for the settlers to breathe. The hot air burned their lungs.

The settlers found the best way to fight fires was to build a firebreak. Quickly, they would take their plow. They would plow several furrows around their house. A furrow is like a long groove. Next, they would burn all the grass in the furrows. This way, when the roaring fire reached the firebreak, it would have nothing to feed on. Then, the settlers would patrol the firebreaks. They would put out hundreds of small fires. Sparks started the small fires. The sparks had jumped the firebreak.

The settlers beat out the small fires quickly. They beat them with blankets or sacks. Sometimes they used animal hides. If they could, they would wet the blankets and sacks. We depend on firefighters to stop fires today. But even today, we do something the early settlers did. Firefighters make firebreaks. They work hard and fast to cut a fire line. They use special tools. They use special equipment. Sometimes they use big digging machines.

Fighting Fire!

After reading the story, answer the questions.
Fill in the circle next to the correct answer.

1. This story is mainly about
   - (a) danger
   - (b) fire and one way to fight it
   - (c) early settlers depending on themselves
   - (d) tools and equipment used by firefighters

2. What answer is in the right order?
   - (a) cut furrows, beat fires with blankets, patrol for fire
   - (b) patrol for fires, beat fires with blankets, cut furrows
   - (c) cut furrows, burn the grass in furrows, patrol for fire
   - (d) burn the grass in furrows, cut furrows, patrol for fire

3. Think about how the word *found* relates to the word *lost*. What words relate in the same way?

   found : lost

   - (a) blanket : wet
   - (b) fast : quickly
   - (c) furrow : groove
   - (d) careless : careful

4. What might make a good firebreak today?
   - (a) a car
   - (b) a road
   - (c) a fence
   - (d) a school

5. Why did the settlers burn the grass in the furrows?
   - (a) So they could patrol the firebreaks.
   - (b) So they could beat out the small fires.
   - (c) So the fire would have nothing to feed on.
   - (d) So the small sparks could jump the firebreak.

Answer Sheets

Student Name: ______________________________

Title of Reading Passage: ______________________________

1. (a) (b) (c) (d) (e)
2. (a) (b) (c) (d) (e)
3. (a) (b) (c) (d) (e)
4. (a) (b) (c) (d) (e)
5. (a) (b) (c) (d) (e)

Student Name: ______________________________

Title of Reading Passage: ______________________________

1. (a) (b) (c) (d) (e)
2. (a) (b) (c) (d) (e)
3. (a) (b) (c) (d) (e)
4. (a) (b) (c) (d) (e)
5. (a) (b) (c) (d) (e)

Bibliography

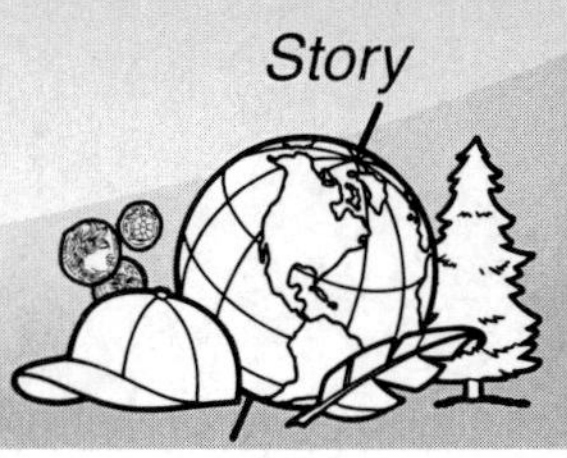

Adair, Gene. *George Washington Carver.* Chelsea House Publishers, 1989.

Alter, Judith. *Growing Up in the Old West.* Franklin Watts, 1989.

"Anthony, Susan B(rownell)" *Encyclopedia Britannica.* Encyclopedia Britannica, Inc., 1990: volume 1, pages 444–445.

Barrett, Tracy. *Growing Up in Colonial America.* The Millbrook Press, Inc., 1995.

Bartoletti, Susan Campbell. *Growing Up in Coal Country.* Houghton Mifflin Company, 1996.

Bial, Raymond. *The Ojibwe.* Marshall Cavendish Corporation, 2000.

Cory, Steve. *Daily Life in Ancient and Modern Mexico.* Runestone Press, The Lerner Publishing Group, 1999.

Davis, Kenneth C. *Don't Know Much About Sitting Bull.* HarperCollins Publishers, 2003.

Donovan, Sandy. *Making Laws: A Look at How a Bill Becomes a Law.* Lerner Publications Company, 2004.

Protecting America: *A Look at the People Who Keep our Country Safe.* Lerner Publications Company, 2004.

Feldman, Ruth Tenzer. *How Congress Works: A Look at the Legislative Branch.* Lerner Publications Company, 2004.

"Fink, Mike" *Encyclopedia Britannica.* Encyclopedia Britannica, Inc., 1990: volume 4, page 782.

Fisher, Leonard Everett. *The Oregon Trail.* Holiday House, Inc., 1990.

Foster, Ruth. *Take Five Minutes: Fascinating Facts About Geography.* Teacher Created Materials, 2003.

——. *Take Five Minutes*: *Fascinating Facts and Stories for Reading and Critical Thinking.* Teacher Created Materials, 2001.

Gaines, Ann. *César E. Chávez: the Fight for Farm Workers' Rights.* The Child's World, 2003.

Gherman, Beverly. *Sandra Day O'Connor.* Viking, Penguin Books, USA Inc., 1991.

Giesecke, Ernestine. *From Seashells to Smart Cards: Money and Currency.* Heinemann Library, Reed Educational & Professional Publishing, 2003.

Gold, Susan Dudley. *Land Pacts.* Twenty-First Century Books, Henry Holt and Company, Inc., 1997.

Gross, Ruth Belov. *True Stories About Abraham Lincoln.* Lothrop, Lee, & Shepard Books, 1973.

Bibliography *(cont.)*

Haugen, Brenda. *Canada ABCs: A Book about the People and Place of Canada.* Picture Window Books, 2004.

Johnson, Sylvia A. *Tomatoes, Potatoes, Corn, and Beans: How the Foods of the Americas Changed Eating Around the World.* Atheneum Books for Young Readers, 1997.

Kellogg, Steven. *Mike Fink.* Scholastic, Inc., 1993.

Knapp, Brian. *The World's Shops and Where They Are.* Grolier Educational Corporation, 1994.

Kramer, Barbara. *Sally Ride: A Space Biography.* Enslow Publishers, Inc., 1998.

Lawlor, Laurie. *Where Will This Shoe Take You?: A Walk Through the History of Footwear.* Walker Publishing Company, Inc., 1996.

"Liberty, Statue of" *Encyclopedia Britannica.* Encyclopedia Britannica, Inc., 1990: volume 7, page 332.

Linz, Kathi. *Chickens May Not Cross the Road and Other Crazy (but True) Laws.* Houghton Mifflin Company, 2002.

Maynard, Charles W. *The Rocky Mountains.* The Rosen Publishing Group, Inc., 2004.

McPherson, Stephanie Sammartino. *The Workers' Detective: A Story about Alice Hamilton.* Carolrhoda Books, Inc., 1992.

Murphy, Andy. *Out and About at the Dairy Farm.* Picture Window Books, 2003.

Oatman, Eric. *Cowboys on the Western Trail: The Cattle Drive Adventures of Joshua McNabb and Davy Bartlett.* National Geographic Society, 2004.

Prevost, John F. *Lake Superior.* ABDO Publishing Company, 2002.

Rasmussen, R. Kent. *Pueblo.* The Rourke Book Company, Inc., 2001.

Schleichert, Elizabeth. *Sitting Bull: Sioux Leader.* Enslow Publishing, Inc., 1997.

Sherrow, Victoria. *Huskings, Quiltings, and Barn Raisings: Work-play Parties in Early America.* Walker Publishing Company, Inc., 1992.

Turner, Robyn Montana. *Dorothea Lange.* Little, Brown, & Company, 1994.

Weidhorn, Manfred. *Jackie Robinson.* Atheneum, Macmillan Publishing Company, 1993.

Wishinsky, Frieda. *What's the Matter with Albert?: A Story of Albert Einstein.* Maple Tree Press, Inc., 2002.

Answer Key

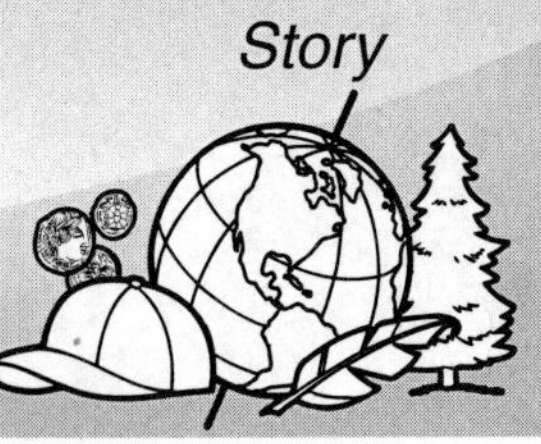

Fishing on a Giraffe's Back
1. d 4. b
2. d 5. a
3. c

Bringing Land to Water
1. d 4. b
2. c 5. b
3. d

A Humbug Insect
1. b 4. b
2. d 5. a
3. a

New Zealand Exchange Student
1. b 4. c
2. a 5. b
3. d

Mike Fink and The Mississippi
1. c 4. c
2. a 5. d
3. a

Not Enough Trees for a House
1. a 4. d
2. b 5. a
3. b

Where Was Ride?
1. c 4. d
2. d 5. a
3. a

One-Room School House
1. d 4. c
2. b 5. b
3. d

A Law About Spinning
1. b 4. a
2. c 5. c
3. a

A Muddy Joke
1. a 4. c
2. a 5. d
3. a

A Spelling Lesson
1. d 4. a
2. b 5. c
3. c

The Ojibwe and Maple Sugar
1. c 4. a
2. b 5. a
3. c

Guts Enough Not to Fight Back
1. b 4. d
2. d 5. a
3. b

Ambulance of the Seas
1. c 4. a
2. a 5. c
3. b

A Supreme Court Case
1. c 4. b
2. b 5. d
3. c

A House Without Doors
1. b 4. a
2. c 5. a
3. c

Pictures that Teach
1. d 4. b
2. d 5. c
3. c

True Stories About Coins
1. c 4. d
2. a 5. b
3. d

The Great Lakes
1. b 4. d
2. a 5. b
3. a

Great Grandpa and the Mine
1. d 4. c
2. c 5. a
3. d

Sitting Bull
1. b 4. c
2. b 5. c
3. d

Arrested for Voting
1. d 4. b
2. b 5. a
3. c

All About Milk
1. c 4. a
2. b 5. d
3. a

A Symbol of Hope
1. b 4. a
2. d 5. d
3. a

Saved from Rabies
1. a 4. c
2. b 5. c
3. d

How Canada Got Its Name
1. c 4. d
2. c 5. b
3. d

Cattle Drive
1. d 4. a
2. a 5. c
3. d

What the President Can't Do
1. c 4. a
2. b 5. d
3. b

"Go for Broke"
1. a 4. a
2. d 5. c
3. b

Tomato Story
1. a 4. c
2. b 5. d
3. b

The Oregon Trail
1. d 4. c
2. d 5. b
3. a

The Man Who Didn't Wear Socks
1. b 4. d
2. c 5. a
3. d

The Underground Railroad
1. d 4. b
2. c 5. a
3. d

A Store Like No Other
1. a 4. d
2. c 5. d
3. b

Following the Crops
1. b 4. c
2. c 5. b
3. d

Seward's Icebox
1. d 4. b
2. b 5. c
3. d

Making Congress Fair
1. c 4. b
2. b 5. a
3. d

Medical Detective
1. a 4. c
2. b 5. c
3. d

What the Shoes Told
1. d 4. d
2. b 5. c
3. a

Work Parties
1. c 4. b
2. a 5. d
3. a

The Rockies
1. a 4. d
2. a 5. c
3. d

Twelve People in a Box
1. c 4. b
2. d 5. a
3. c

True Stories About Money
1. c 4. a
2. b 5. a
3. d

Fighting Fire!
1. b 4. b
2. c 5. c
3. d